The Official 411

Degrassi GENERATIONS

Kathryn Ellis | Introduction by Kevin Smith

New York | London | Toronto | Sydney

A Pocket Books / Madison Press Book

POCKET BOOKS, a division of Simon & Schuster, Inc.
1230 Avenue of the Americas, New York, NY 10020

ISBN-13: 978-1-4165-1680-4
ISBN-10: 1-4165-1680-8

First Pocket Books trade paperback edition September 2005

10 9 8 7 6 5 4 3 2 1

Manufactured in Singapore

For information regarding special discounts for bulk purchases, please contact
Simon & Schuster Special Sales at 1-800-456-6798 or business@simonandschuster.com

Cover images: © Barbara Cole

Produced by Madison Press Books
1000 Yonge Street, Suite 200
Toronto, Ontario, Canada M4W 2K2
www.madisonpressbooks.com

CONTENTS

PREFACE

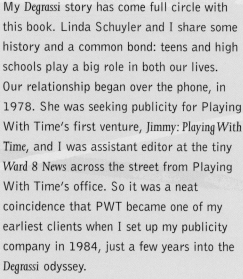

Kathryn Ellis is a long-time *Degrassi* insider. She handled all publicity and promotion for the original *Degrassi* series and wrote five of the episodes. She is also the author of two *Degrassi* novels and has appeared on the series as an extra. She lives in Toronto, not far from Degrassi Street.

My *Degrassi* story has come full circle with this book. Linda Schuyler and I share some history and a common bond: teens and high schools play a big role in both our lives. Our relationship began over the phone, in 1978. She was seeking publicity for Playing With Time's first venture, *Jimmy: Playing With Time*, and I was assistant editor at the tiny *Ward 8 News* across the street from Playing With Time's office. So it was a neat coincidence that PWT became one of my earliest clients when I set up my publicity company in 1984, just a few years into the *Degrassi* odyssey.

As publicist for the show, I had the opportunity to be everywhere. I was in the loop on story, so I could get my press materials ready. I was in the stills archives, in the office, and I got to hang out on set at times. I dealt with the media and the public. I interviewed the young actors for press kits, took them to media interviews, and had the chance to travel out of town with them. Sometimes, I even found myself

in the editing room or at a mixing session. And of course, I am married to Yan Moore, the principal writer for *Degrassi Classic*. While writing one episode per year for *Degrassi Junior High* and *Degrassi High*, I was able to learn about the scriptwriting process first hand, and I did research on the issues. I was asked to write *Degrassi* novels and to create and oversee the production of other *Degrassi* print materials.

I have since left publicity for teaching (I was bored without teenagers around.), but Yan's work on the early years of *Degrassi: The Next Generation* kept me in the know. All of this has given me both a microscope and a telescope to view so much that is *Degrassi*.

That's me playing an audience member on DJH!

DEGRASSI

And what is *Degrassi*? It is unique in being a show with two incarnations inhabiting the same world at different times. It's a television show that seems to have captured the spirit of growing up for two separate generations, igniting a fierce loyalty among its audience. Viewers seem to take the show to heart and are often surprised to find so many others out there who feel the same way.

    Degrassi: Generations is a celebration of this twenty-five-year-old TV franchise. Thank you for letting me be your host. I have never had so much fun as I had collecting what follows. What a pleasure to reconnect with so many of the old gang, both cast and crew. I'm only sorry I couldn't touch base with everyone. What fun it has been to meet all the fabulous new cast members! How fascinating to get to know the current crew and find out how they put together the new show. And to connect with so many viewers — without all of you, there would have been no point in any of us showing up to work every day.

    If you are mentioned anywhere in this book, either by name or as part of a group,

please consider this book my thank you — every one of you, without a single exception, has helped make it easier — or even possible — to put all this together. We've tried to thank everyone involved with this project in another part of this book, but here I must thank my lovely husband Yan, without whose support this book could not have been written. Or, I would have disintegrated into tiny, unrecognizable pieces. Or, I would have starved to death. Most likely all three.

— *Toronto*, 2005

INTRODUCTION

Kevin Smith's film credits include *Mallrats*, *Chasing Amy*, *Dogma*, and *Jay and Silent Bob Strike Back*. His fans have made a game of spotting the *Degrassi* references in his work.

Like any good fairy tale, this one ends with a Canadian chick's tongue in my mouth.

I'd been a fan of *Degrassi Junior High* and *Degrassi High* since the early nineties, when poor reception on an ol' rabbit-eared portable TV in a convenience store brought this teen soap operatic gem from the True North to my attention, and I very quickly fell in love with not only the trials and tribulations of this rag-tag band of Toronto youngsters, but also their adorable accents ("aboot" and the like). But the lion's share of said affection was reserved solely for one distaff Canuck in the cast in particular: the little epileptic girl with the fierce principles and the penchant for dudes in fedoras.

Her name was Caitlin Ryan.

Caitlin Ryan was the girl of my dreams: she was smart, soulful, beautiful, socially-conscious, and handicapped (if, indeed, epilepsy can be categorized as handicapped). That combination meant that she could stand on her own two feet, yet still needed to be cared for and protected from the cruel, harsh world as well.

And make no mistake about it: Degrassi was, indeed, a cruel and harsh world. Chicks were getting pregnant, guys were running away from home, and little dudes were mystified by wet dreams. This was a school so tough that even the bully was reduced to tears (by AIDS, no less). And that's what made the fictional secondary school (and the show it was named after) so identifiable and habit-forming: *Degrassi* held up a mirror to schools the world over and reflected the highs and lows of the adolescent denizens that populate their hallways. What Linda Schuyler and company managed to do was present youth culture with a show about them and for them that didn't condescend, mock, or wrap things up in a neat little bow at the end of twenty-two minutes. I never thought any TV program would come close to achieving that magic again...

Until *Degrassi: The Next Generation*.

TNG was everything that *Degrassi Classic* was, plus more. The kids of Degrassi were still getting into trouble of all kinds but now they were dressed better, were played by more convincing actors, and honored their origins by including the trailblazers who'd roamed the halls a decade plus before. And this meant that my crush was still in the house.

Yes — Caitlin Ryan had grown up.

And like a teenager who never forgets his first love, I used what little clout I had in the movie industry to do what every guy with a crush on a fictional character would do: I guest-starred on three episodes as an unmarried and childless version of myself who comes to Toronto with Jason Mewes to shoot a flick called *Jay and Silent Bob Go Canadian, Eh!*, during which I meet and fall for local journalist Caitlin Ryan. I even managed to get a kissing scene for the fake version of myself, thus forever shattering the thin membrane between a TV reality and the real world. So after thirteen years of fandom, I got to play tonsil-hockey with the Canadian girl of my dreams.

And that's a testimony to the power of the *Degrassi* mythos: it's a crafted world that's so real, you can get sucked in. For a quarter century, *Degrassi* has helped youngsters (and sometimes adults) through the awkward phase of going from kids to teens to grownups. It's a show so convincing in its earnestness that one never doubts its sincerity. And in today's post-modern, self-aware culture, that's as rare as a kid at Degrassi with no issues or problems.

I'd like to think somewhere, in one of the dozens of countries the show is now seen, there's a kid harboring a crush on a current *Degrassi* character. And if, like me, he or she is nursing fantasies about one day bombing around the halls of Degrassi and interacting with those fictional kids, I wanna let 'em know that they should never give up their dream — because whatever it takes, *Degrassi* will see you through.

And, who knows? Maybe one day, you too will find yourself being frenched by a *Degrassi* girl.

— Kevin Smith, *Los Angeles*, 2005

Chapter 1

THE DEGRASSI STORY

The headquarters of ➔
Playing With Time

It all began, fittingly enough, in a school. In 1979, Linda Schuyler was a grade seven and eight teacher at Earl Grey Senior Public School in Toronto. She encouraged her students to use video to tell stories. She had also produced a few documentary films on her own and then with her partner, Kit Hood, at their recently formed production company, Playing With Time (PWT). Linda's pal and Earl Grey's librarian, Bruce Mackey, knew of her interest in getting kids to make films and ordered every book he could find on the subject. When the book *Ida Makes a Movie* arrived, he laughed with Linda at his mistake. What could a senior public school library do with a kids' book about cats making a movie?

LINDA SCHUYLER
Executive Producer, Epitome Pictures

As a partner in Playing With Time, Inc. and later Epitome Pictures, Linda has been the constant force behind the world of *Degrassi*.

ON WHAT SETS THE SHOW APART

Good, human storytelling. And it's Canadian! A big difference is we cast age-appropriate actors. The kids aren't bringing more world experience to the characters than they have. When twenty-year-olds are playing fifteen-year-olds, they've got five extra years of life experience and that does make a difference. There's also the double mandate of entertainment and education. In the *Degrassi* world, there are consequences.

ON WHAT SHE IS MOST PROUD OF

We say that if kids are talking about it in the schoolyard, it should be all right for us to talk about it on television. I'm very proud of the stories we've done on issues like abortion, teen suicide, and oral sex. Even though we are creating a show for young people, we are getting a much farther reach than we intended. Winning a

The school library had no use for the book, but PWT did. After meeting with lawyer Stephen Stohn for advice, Linda went to New York to see Kay Chorao, the book's author. A deal was struck and Linda and Kit began work on their first fiction film. The cats became kids, the book became a script, and the first step was taken on what would become a very long street that stretched ahead through the years and around the world.

Grants and loans funded the movie project. Amy Jo Cooper, PWT's office assistant, wrote the script and Philip Earnshaw, a recent film school grad with whom Linda had worked on a documentary, was brought on board to operate the camera. Auditions were held, the young actors were cast, and Bruce offered his house as a location. (That's his dog, Ryan, you can see on the lawn in the film.) As producer, Linda took on all kinds of tasks, from sandwich maker to driver.

Kay Chorao has written and illustrated over eighty books. Among her earliest are *A Magic Eye for Ida* and its sequel, *Ida Makes a Movie*, which was adapted for the first episode of *The Kids of Degrassi Street.*

Gemini for best children's show and also for the best dramatic show in Canada made me very proud. But I would say that my favorite moments are when we get "Dear Degrassi" letters, in which people just say, "Thank you," for a specific episode about something they've lived through personally or that they're living through with their own children.

ON THAT SPECIAL QUALITY

The shows can't have lost what they originally had, because I don't think you'd get 2,000 kids lining up at the mall to meet the actors if they had. There's something special about a *Degrassi* show that you just don't get in other shows. But I had the same nervousness when we started *The Next Generation* as I did the first time. I was so afraid that we couldn't capture lightning in a bottle twice. I spent the first season of filming on TNG in complete fear. I worried that people would say, "Why didn't you just let it go?"

ON MOVING TO THE EPITOME STUDIOS

I was nervous about doing TNG as a studio show. Set Designer Tamara Deverell and I did a lot of research. But since, I've heard of teachers who sit in staff rooms arguing about which school it's shot in! People don't know it's a studio show!

On September 20, 1980, the Canadian Broadcasting Corporation aired "Ida Makes a Movie." The next year, CBC ordered two more shows from PWT, "Cookie Goes to Hospital" and "Irene Moves In." By 1982, CBC had recognized a good thing and ordered five new episodes. Kit and Linda hired Sari Friedland as production manager and chose Yan Moore, a young film editor, to be their picture editor. When "Casey Draws the Line" ran into story problems, Yan — in a light bulb moment riding home on the streetcar — figured out a solution. He wrote some new scenes for the episode and launched his *Degrassi* writing career. Together, the seven episodes were called *The Kids of Degrassi Street*.

The final six episodes of *KDS* aired in 1985. The season was dubbed "Yearbook" and shows the class's efforts to put together the yearbook as a continuing thread. "Yearbook" became an experiment that looked ahead to *Degrassi Junior High*, which writer Avrum Jacobson was hired to develop.

The episode "Griff Makes a Date" grabbed some serious attention from award-giving bodies, although awards had been collecting on the PWT shelves since "Ida." National media attention was starting to grow. In 1986, "Griff Gets a Hand" took the prestigious Prix Jeunesse and the International Emmy for Best Program for Children and Young People.

At the same time, auditions were being held for *Degrassi Junior High*. The first kid to bounce through the door was Pat Mastroianni, the future Joey Jeremiah. The Repertory Company of fifty-four kids was formed. *DJH* was produced in association with CBC and Kate Taylor of PBS flagship station WGBH.

At the end of the first season of *DJH*, the character Spike fears she is pregnant. The producers were so nervous about this groundbreaking story line, they shot two endings to the scene.

In 1987, the series won Gemini Awards for Children's Series and a directing nod for Kit Hood, and another International Emmy — this time for "It's Late," Spike's pregnancy episode. Accepting the Emmy, Kit announced that if Spike's baby were a boy, it would be named after the president of the Academy of Television Arts and Sciences, Ralph Baruch. It was then quickly decided that the baby would be a girl, Emma — after the Emmy.

DJH began airing in the U.S. on various PBS stations in 1988. Fan mail, press attention, awards, and accolades were on the rise.

As the kids grew up, the series morphed into *Degrassi High*. By now, there were over one million viewers per episode in Canada. The show was being distributed to countries around the world, including Australia and Britain.

The final season of DH was shot in 1990. PWT ended the series with a TV movie. While it was in development, PWT went on the road across Canada to film six issues-based, nonfiction shows called *Degrassi Talks*.

On January 5, 1992, *School's Out!* shocked its

KIT HOOD
Director and Producer, Degrassi Classic

Kit's career in the world of entertainment began when he was a child, working as an actor. That led to an interest in filmmaking. He co-founded Playing With Time with Linda. The company was named after their first documentary about a marathon piano player, *Jimmy: Playing with Time*.

ON THE ROLLER COASTER

The start of each new season was like climbing aboard a huge roller coaster. It was exhilarating, but I was relieved when the ride stopped. Some new element was added each season to keep the ride exciting; but the season always started before these parts could be tested. I was usually scared that something would break. Seems silly now, especially when everything worked out as intended.

ON THE REST OF THE TEAM

We were a tight group. We developed good ideas in a mutually supportive environment and struggled with the ups and downs of film production with shared optimism.

ON HIS LIFE NOW

My life has gone on from *Degrassi* in a unique direction that wasn't what I had anticipated fifteen years ago. I'm doing very well! I live on about fifty acres on the Atlantic Ocean, not far from Halifax, Nova Scotia. Wildlife surrounds me, the landscape is beautiful, and I have many new interests.

STEPHEN STOHN
Executive Vice President, Epitome Pictures

As DJH became more successful, a lawyer was needed. Who better than the young man who gave Linda some free legal advice before her seminal meeting with Kay Chorao? To this day, Stephen continues to handle the show's legal affairs. He also contributes creatively to *Degrassi*, co-writing the show's theme song and producing the Degrassi.tv Web site.

ON HIS CREATIVE CONTRIBUTIONS

My interest really starts to perk up once the show is shot. In post-production, the sound is something I love. I'm definitely

Ivan Fecan was director of television programming at CBC from 1987 to 1991. He oversaw *Degrassi*'s move to prime time because it "spoke equally to teens and parents," recalls Fecan. By 1994, he had joined CTV. Not surprisingly, he was excited when *TNG* was created.

2.4 million viewers when Snake and Caitlin used the f-word. *Degrassi* had said goodbye with one more controversy to its credit. As a testament to the show's impact, and also for her volunteer work on various committees, in 1994, Linda was made a Member of the Order of Canada, one of the highest honors that can be awarded to a Canadian civilian.

In the years that followed, the players went off in many directions. Linda established a new partnership with Stephen Stohn and founded Epitome Pictures. Kit became a gentleman farmer, first on Salt Spring Island, British Columbia, and later in Nova Scotia. Meanwhile, the *Degrassi Classic* shows were alive and well in reruns and in schools.

In 1999, a televised reunion special on CBC's *Jonovision* brought some of the *Degrassi* cast back together. The special was so popular, Yan and Linda thought maybe it was time for a reunion of the fictitious *Degrassi High* characters, too. When Yan did the math, he realized that baby Emma would just be entering junior high school.

Ivan Fecan, CEO of Canadian broadcaster CTV's parent company, ordered thirteen episodes of *Degrassi: The Next Generation.*

an audio person. Music isn't just what interests me in the show, but the entire sound design.

ON BEING A MANAGER

Morale is a hard thing to build up; it's great when you've got it, and it's easy to lose. A big part of it is hiring the right people, listening to problems, and giving the right feedback. The other part is making decisions. I don't think it can be underestimated how important it is to make decisions quickly, firmly, and to take responsibility for them.

ON THE FUN PART

As executive producer of the Web site, once a day I go to this particular thread called Shooting Season Three. It's up to about 25,000 posts now. People ask questions and I post updates. I enjoy interacting with the viewers, sometimes creating a little contest, giving away some t-shirts or memorabilia.

Phil returned in the role of director for some episodes. The brand-new cable channel The N came on board to broadcast TNG in the U.S., thanks to Director of Programming Meeri Cunniff's memories of *Degrassi Classic* as the perfect teen show.

The new show went on the air in January 2001 and took off, winning Geminis each year and growing a fan base in Canada, the U.S., Australia, New Zealand, and many more countries, just like the old show. The 2003 season began with Emma searching for her father. The "old" *Degrassi* characters — Joey, Caitlin, Snake, and Spike — became more prominent, with story lines of their own. The mix seemed to appeal to the audience, many of whom had been fans of the *Degrassi Classic* series. Pregnancy and abortion story lines and a gay teen kiss stirred up the trademark *Degrassi* controversy yet again. There are always issues to explore. Who knows what's still in store for the *Degrassi* characters?

THE PLAYING WITH TIME
REPERTORY COMPANY

Unique among Canadian television shows, *Degrassi Junior High* drew its cast from a repertory company. Flyers and notices in Toronto papers attracted more than 500 applications from children all over the city. From these, 300 auditioned and fifty were selected for a three-week workshop. After the three weeks, the first roles were cast. Each season and on into *Degrassi High*, about twenty more kids would go through the workshops and a handful would be added to the cast. A few would leave each season for various reasons, but the repertory company grew a little every year. In total, about sixty-five kids were "Repco" over the years.

The workshops helped the young actors overcome self-consciousness and develop concentration, imagination, and verbal and physical acting skills. Instructors used acting exercises and improvisation. The kids also had seminars in filmmaking, including how a camera works and what editing is all about. Kids who had been through a season with the series were placed in more advanced workshops where they worked on their personal performance goals.

Characters were developed by the production and writing team based on the strengths of the actors, and actors who showed promise sometimes had roles developed or expanded for them. A discussion was held after the first read-through of each script and the kids' input was actively sought. The team listened to the kids' comments, ad libs, and concerns — they even eavesdropped on their conversations. Often, an element from one of the kids' own lives — such as getting glasses or going joyriding — was incorporated in the plot.

Although some characters were seen more often in episodes, everyone in the Repco had equal status. They all had to put in their time as background characters — it's not unusual to see major characters in the background of a scene on *Degrassi Classic* — nearly unheard-of on other television shows. Any actor could be plucked from the background and given lines or even a full part.

A number of the members earned school credits for being in the Repco, but all of them had to keep up with their school work. No one needed to miss more than eight days of school in any month — another advantage of working with a rep company system. When *Degrassi*'s first incarnation ended, Playing With Time set up The PWT Foundation, to which any Repco member could apply to fund further education, a film project, or any kind of project that would help their futures — and many did.

Modern professional television does not allow for a repertory company system, but there are many holdovers from the Repco days. Just like the old series, *Degrassi: The Next Generation* has workshops at the beginning of each season. The episodes still change their focus from character to character each week; discussion and input from the actors is still valued; and conversations still attract eavesdroppers!

a DAY

ON SET WITH TWO STARS OF DEGRASSI

Who: Pat Mastroianni
Character: Joey Jeremiah
Series: Degrassi Junior High
When: September 03, 1988
Episode: "Twenty Bucks"

1988

THE SCENES: 1 / 27 / 28

Caitlin discovers her date with Joey is part of a bet. She angrily dumps Coke on him and runs off. Joey tears up the money he's won from the bet to prove his feelings are genuine.

Instead of filming at the school, these scenes were filmed at night inside and outside a restaurant.

Pat Mastroianni
a.k.a. Joey Jeremiah

2004

Miriam McDonald
a.k.a. Emma Nelson

Who: Miriam McDonald
Character: Emma Nelson
Series: Degrassi The Next Gen.
When: September 01, 2004
Episode: "Secret, Parts 1 & 2"

THE SCENES: 4 / 17 / 101

Emma needs to pull up her marks. Jay and Alex are still an item. A gonorrhea outbreak spreads through the school. Tension builds between Jay and Emma. Emma gives Nate a kiss.

It was a fairly typical filming day at Epitome. Scenes 4 and 17 were filmed in Studio A. Scene 101 took place in Studio C. The crew took advantage of a long day of natural summer light.

in the LIFE THEN & NOW

12:30 p.m. Pat has arrived early, in costume. He chats about the new car battery he bought for his 1975 Impala. Pat is needed on set.

1:00 p.m. Scene 1 is rehearsed.

1:15 p.m. Polaroid pictures are taken of the actors, in case a scene needs to be partly reshot. Polaroids are kept for reference.

1:30 p.m. The first actual take.

1:40 p.m. The crew prepares for the second set-up, a "reverse angle." Pat checks his hair and costume in the mirror.

1:45 p.m. A sound problem arises: the hum of the neon is audible on the recording. The crew tries to muffle the sound.

1:55 p.m. The problem is solved. The sound recordist tapes some "room tone" so that viewers

8:10 a.m. Miriam arrives. She gets into costume.

8:30 a.m. She has her hair done and chats with Mike (Jay).

9:11 a.m. Miriam plays a round of pool with Mike.

9:15 a.m. The crew sets up lights. Jake (Craig) and Mike discuss, and then play, a CD by Hawksley Workman.

9:40 a.m. They are called to set to rehearse. Hair touch-ups are made.

9:50 a.m. Shot 97 Take 1

9:52 a.m. Eleanore Lindo directs. She likes the emotion, but wants more energy.

9:53 a.m. 97 Take 2; 97 Take 3.

10:00 a.m. Rehearsal. Two takes are done. Miriam breaks while lighting is adjusted. Stand-ins are used and the floor is tape marked for accuracy.

10:16 a.m. Rehearsal is done.

10:18 a.m. Shot 99 Take 1. A horn blasts and red lights

flash as a warning not to walk in or make noise that would ruin the take. (Film stock and crew time are expensive.) A double horn blast means "cut."

10:20 a.m. The lens is checked for hair or dust and a bell indicates "the gate is clean."

10:40 a.m. The crew relocates and sets up while the actors eat a snack. Miriam changes costume and hair and then surfs the Web to pass time.

Pat Mastroianni

Series: Degrassi Junior High

Director John Bertram

don't notice a sudden silence.

2:00 p.m. The actors break while the crew sets up. A snack is served.

2:20 p.m. They run through the reverse angle. Pat waits for his cue. The shot goes smoothly.

2:30 p.m. The crew prepares for a wider shot of the same angle.

3:15 p.m. Scene 1 is complete.

3:20 p.m. Tech check. The actors change costume.

3:35 p.m. The first run-through of Scene 27 begins.

3:55 p.m. The scene is still being rehearsed. New extras are used. The scene is run through up to the point before Caitlin dumps the Coke on Joey — there's no need to get him wet before it's shot!

4:00 p.m. Finally, it's a take and Caitlin dumps the "Coke" — water dyed with food coloring. The director yells, "Cut!" and everyone bursts out laughing.

4:02 p.m. Pat quickly changes into a second sweatshirt. His

hair is dried for another take.

4:04 p.m. A third sweatshirt and another blow-dry. The extras are dismissed. The crew sets up for the reverse angle.

4:30 p.m. For this angle, they film up to the dumping.

5:55 p.m. The actual dumping is filmed.

6:05 p.m. Stacie and Pat repeat the scene for the still photographer. Stacie just keeps dumping Coke after Coke on Pat.

11:30 a.m. She is called to set.

12:30 p.m. A close-up of Miriam's bracelet is shot. Actors pass by even though just their reflections will be seen on the glossy floor beyond her.

12:47 p.m. The scene is done!

12:50 p.m. Miriam shows Ryan (J.T.) some dance steps and jumps. She checks her lines.

1:10 p.m. Miriam's costume and hair are changed. The gang is called to set for

another rehearsal.

1:18 p.m. Makeup is fixed.

1:25 p.m. A second take begins.

1:35 p.m. Lunch is announced. The actors mimic the crew, "Don't touch anything! Hot set!" They'll be filming more of the same scene after lunch.

1:45 p.m. Miriam chooses food from the buffet in the lunch room — the school cafeteria when that location is needed. She opts for lunch in the sun.

2:10 p.m. Miriam cools off with a Popsicle and wanders around the outdoor set.

2:30 p.m. Miriam brushes her teeth.

2:40 p.m. Back on set, she gives her lines and reactions. Waiting, measuring for focus, close-ups of various actors in the scene, and yet another angle — and then more Popsicles! One more angle is taken, and the gate is clean.

6:20 p.m. Pat can get dried off. He changes into his own clothes, but he hasn't got spare underwear — and he is wet!

6:45 p.m. Pat is stopped on his way back to the office by some fans asking for his autograph.

7:00 p.m. All the actors are sent home except Pat, Stacie, and two extras who go for dinner.

8:15 p.m. Pat and Stacie are ready to shoot the night scene, but it has started to rain. The crew is busy building a track for the camera to roll along during a "tracking" shot. A huge umbrella has been unfolded over the camera.

8:30 p.m. The art director arrives with raincoats and rain hats for Pat and Stacie to wear during run-throughs.

9:00 p.m. Pat and Stacie wait for some adjustments.

9:05 p.m. Pat is given a new sweatshirt to wear with a much more noticeable stain.

9:15 p.m. Another run-through, a real take, then a snack.

10:05 p.m. A reverse-angle take. Pat quickly blow-dries his hair for a shot of Stacie and himself arriving at the restaurant.

10:20 p.m. It's a wrap.

10:25 p.m. Pat calls his mom to let her know he's on his way. He's worried -— his new car battery isn't in yet, and with this rain, the Impala might not start.

10:30 p.m. Back in his own clothes, Pat tries his car and — yes — it starts!

4:20 p.m. Everybody relocates for the last scene of the day. A school bus that is needed for the shot won't start, so the crew rolls it into position. Lighting is discussed. Early evening light is beginning and the scene is not finished. Miriam dashes off to get changed for the final scene.

5:00 p.m. Rehearsals.

5:10 p.m. The shot is filmed with the camera on a dolly.

5:20 p.m. Polaroid pictures are taken to ensure continuity.

5:24 p.m. As a plane flies over, the sound crew asks for a pause before the shot is made.

5:30 p.m. A new setup and more takes are completed.

5:40 p.m. A snack of nachos is brought out for cast and crew.

5:50 p.m. A second part of the scene is prepared while Miriam hangs out with Cassie (Manny).

6:10 p.m. Another angle is shot. First Assistant Director Derby Crewe gives a few instructions.

6:38 p.m. Miriam and Jonathan (Nate) rehearse, without the kiss.

7:00 p.m. Even though Miriam's part is finished filming, she stays for Cassie's close-up.

7:15 p.m. It's a wrap! Miriam grabs a drink, changes back into her own clothes, and signs out. She gets her call sheet for the next day and heads off.

STORY LINES &
SCRIPTS

Chapter 2

There would be no _Degrassi_ without the creative talents of the members of the writing department who have given the characters their stories and voices. Before the directors, actors, and all of the rest of the people you will meet later in this book can work their magic, there must be a story to tell.

Writers on THE KIDS OF DEGRASSI STREET

Susan A'Court • John Bertram • Amy Jo Cooper • Michelle Dionne • Yan Moore

Writers on DEGRASSI CLASSIC

Scott Barrie • Kathryn Ellis • Avrum Jacobson • Michael Kennedy • Yan Moore • Susin Nielsen • John Oughton

Writers on DEGRASSI: TNG

Tassie Cameron • Sean Carley • Craig Cornell • Claire Ross Dunn • James Hurst • Sean Jara • Aaron Martin • Yan Moore • Susin Nielsen • Miklos Perlus • Shelley Scarrow • Rebecca Schechter • Jana Sinyor • David Sutherland • Brendon Yorke

YAN MOORE
Co-Creator and Creative Consultant, TNG

Yan was one of the first students to graduate from Queen's University with a degree in Film Studies. He landed a job as a picture editor at Playing With Time. By the time _DJH_ was in full swing, Yan was the show's head writer. After _School's Out!_, Yan worked on other shows, but _Degrassi_ has a way of holding on to people.

ON WHERE THE IDEAS COME FROM

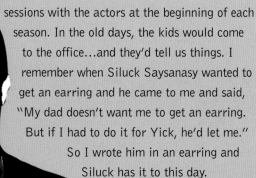

From everywhere! Our own teenage years, magazines and newspapers, conversations overheard, official idea sessions with the actors at the beginning of each season. In the old days, the kids would come to the office...and they'd tell us things. I remember when Siluck Saysanasy wanted to get an earring and he came to me and said, "My dad doesn't want me to get an earring. But if I had to do it for Yick, he'd let me." So I wrote him in an earring and Siluck has it to this day.

AARON MARTIN
Executive Producer (Creative), TNG

Aaron had recently graduated from the Canadian Film Centre in Toronto when he joined TNG at the beginning and the reins were passed fully to him by the third season. Aaron ensures that the scripts are consistent and high quality and he writes some of those scripts himself.

ON HIS WRITING ROUTINE

I need pressure, so I tend to write...not last minute, but I need that ticking clock. I usually write from 2 p.m. to about 2 a.m. I like the TV being on; I like distractions. I tend to write a ton of stuff and then go back and rewrite it.

ON ISSUES

If it's a hard-hitting issue, like cutting, date rape, or abortion, we have to make sure that our research is there, and there entirely, and that we're telling the right story. *Degrassi* might be the first time the viewers have ever explored some of these issues.

ON ADVICE FOR YOUNG WRITERS

I always go back to story. Make sure you know what you're telling, and listen to people's criticism. Go to school. The Film Centre was great for me. The other thing is that you have to realize that only a few people get to do it and you have to be that dedicated.

ON THE DIFFERENCES BETWEEN THE OLD AND NEW SHOWS

The new show is slicker, with snappier dialogue and a hipper look. On the old show, when we started out, there were only a few of us and Phil was virtually lighting with flashlights; whereas, on the new show, you can barely move without tripping over lights and crew. But at the heart, I see much of the same — capturing the world of kids and reassuring them they're not alone. Could *Degrassi* once again capture the "Zit-geist?" I think they have.

THE RULES

OF WRITING DEGRASSI CLASSIC

1 Each episode has an A plot, a B plot, and a C plot. The A plot will come to some sort of resolution by the end of the episode. The action of the story takes place within a week.

2 The B plot should have some connection to the A plot.

3 The C plot may be setting up or finishing off events in other episodes, or may simply be providing comic relief.

4 The opening 30 to 60 second teaser has to set up the A plot, let the viewer know what issues or themes the episode will tackle, and end with a kicker.

5 After the opening sequence, the action always takes place at school, in the A plot.

6 There is a crisis at the midpoint for the commercial out.

7 Adults are never seen in a scene without a *Degrassi* kid present. Very rare exceptions have been made to this rule (only two in total).

8 No preaching.

9 No WIBNIs (wouldn't-it-be-neat-ifs) — meaning no writing things that really couldn't happen in real life.

10 Show ends in a freeze on the character from the A plot who learned something.

OF WRITING DEGRASSI: TNG

1 Every episode has an A plot and a subordinate B plot. The A plot is usually about one character dealing with one issue.

2 The B plot is usually more comedic, though not always. Often, B plots move season-long story arcs forward.

3 Sometimes there will be a C plot, or the thread of a larger, season-long arc in the episode.

4 The teaser is always from the A plot.

5 Act 1 (the scene after the opening credits) is always an A plot scene.

6 Act 1 always ends on an A plot scene.

7 Act 2 (after the first commercial break) can start on either the A or B plot.

8 Act 2 always ends on an A plot scene.

9 The Tag (after the final commercial break) always starts on the B plot, and ends on the A plot. Sometimes the Tag is A plot only. The A plot character always gets the coveted freeze at the end of the episode.

By 1992, Canadian televison viewers had heard the f-word in the occasional documentary, but it had never been used in a prime-time drama. Why did Yan Moore decide to use it in *School's Out!*?

"There was a tension growing, especially between Joey and Snake," recalls Yan. "Snake had this tremendous frustration and the word had never been used in a script before. So, when Snake finally lost it with Joey, the word was included. Since Caitlin overheard the conversation, it just seemed right for her to use that totally unCaitlin-like word.... It was expected that the CBC would say, 'No, you can't do it,' but bless them, they

%$#*!

saw that it was the right word. It was something no one would expect to hear on a Sunday night on CBC!"

Stefan Brogren, as Snake, was tremedously excited about becoming the first person to say the f-word on Canadian televison. "I took pride in that," he says today. "I couldn't believe we got away with it, to tell you the truth.... We said, 'Are they going to...let us...do this? Is it actually going to make it in?' Because it was shocking. Now, they show movies on some stations unedited, but back then it was a big deal."

Snake: Let's recap the Jeremiah summer, shall we? See what a swell and decent human being you've been.

Joey: I don't have to listen to this!

Snake: No, you're going to listen to me. [Caitlin enters, unseen by Snake.] Joey Jeremiah spends his summer dating Caitlin...

Joey: Shut up!

Snake: And f---ing Tessa. Oh, what ethics! Oh, what a hero! Let's have a great big hand, shall we? Big round of applause, eh? Yes, alright! [Snake sees Caitlin, exits.]

Joey: Snake's got a fairly weird sense of humor.

Caitlin: Tessa Campanelli? You were f---ing Tessa Campanelli?

SCREENWRITING: A HOW-TO

If you'd like to write your own episode of *Degrassi*, you need to start with the story idea. Begin in point form; don't try to write a real script yet.

STEP 1: OUTLINE THE STORY

1   Choose a character you'd like to tell a story about. If you want, make up a character of your own — it can even be yourself. Give the character a personality.

2   What is that character's goal? Think about your favorite movies, books, plays, and TV shows; what do the protagonists want? Dorothy wants to get home from Oz. Romeo and Juliet want to get married. Joey wants to make a video.

3   Put an obstacle in the character's way. Dorothy doesn't know how to get home.

Romeo's and Juliet's parents hate each other. Joey doesn't have a video camera.

4   Now, push your character to find a solution. Dorothy sets off to find the Wizard. Juliet gets her nurse to hook her up with Romeo. Joey tries to persuade Lucy to film the video.

5   See what your character encounters in attempting to achieve the goal. Dorothy makes some friends. Romeo and Juliet get married in secret. Lucy condemns the content of the video as anti-feminist and won't work with Clutch, who owns the splatter car to be used in the video.

6   How does it all turn out? Dorothy finally makes it home. Romeo and Juliet die. Joey gets his video — for a price.

STEP 2: SCENE BREAKDOWN

Whenever you change location or time of day, it's a new scene. Write out each scene describing where it takes place and what happens in it. Remember, each scene needs a reason to be in the story. Where the outline told us what the story is, the scene breakdown tells us how it happens. Keep your character's personality in mind so that your scenes are believable.

STEP 3: FIRST DRAFT

Try your hand at a first draft. Fill in what the characters will say in the scene, using action and dialogue to reveal what's going on in their heads. If you keep thinking about what kind of person your character is, you will get believable dialogue. But even if you don't think it's very good at first, don't stop writing. If you're not sure where to start, ask yourself, Who would speak first? What would that character say? How would the other character answer? You can always go back and fix it later, but at least you've started.

STEP 4: SHOWTIME!

Professional screenwriters will polish their material at every step along the way, with input from producers, broadcasters, and sometimes directors and actors. So, it's time to get your friends to read the script aloud in order to get some input. You may even want to get costumes, find locations, and film your script with a video camera.

STEP 5: AFTERWARD

Many people enjoy writing fan fiction and some of it is pretty good. But there's no point in sending it to a show's producers because, let's face it, they'll never look at it! They are unable to view other writers' material, in case they themselves are pursuing a similar story line. So post it on fan sites, or just enjoy the experience of writing for yourself and with your friends. If you want to be a pro yourself, there's just one thing to do — keep writing! You can take classes, get feedback from friends and professionals, read books on writing, and work your way toward the television writers' table. Every writer's journey is unique, but each one of them who got there just kept writing — and never gave up!

Chapter 3

CHARACTERS & ACTORS

Strong story lines and realistic portrayals are the hallmarks of *Degrassi*. Meet the *Degrassi* family of characters, and the actors who play them.

THE KIDS OF DEGRASSI STREET

The Kids of Degrassi Street was a series of stand-alone, half-hour mini-movies that focused on everyday dilemmas in ordinary kids' lives. Each episode's title told the viewer who the central character would be. These characters all lived on Degrassi Street and attended the same school. Some were siblings, some were friends, and some barely knew each other.

THE CAST OF KIDS

Ryan Anderson (Ryan)

Genevieve Appleton (Liz)

Danah-Jean Brown (Connie)

Christopher Charlesworth (Benjamin)

Sarah Charlesworth (Casey)

Peter Duckworth Pilkington III (Noel)

Nick Goddard (Chuck)

Anais Granofsky (Karen)

Stacey Halberstadt (Sophie)

Dawn Harrison (Catherine "Cookie")

Neil Hope (Robin "Griff")

John Ioannou (Pete)

Nancy Lam (Irene)

Arlene Lott (Rachel)

Stacie Mistysyn (Lisa)

Zoe Newman (Ida)

Matthew Roberts (Jeffrey)

Tanya Schmalfuss (Samantha)

Jamie Summerfield (Martin)

Tyson Talbot (Billy)

MORE KIDS IN FEATURED ROLES

Rachel Blanchard (Melanie)

Kelvin Chin (Lin)

Corey Goodman (Tom)

Robyn Harrison (Terri)

Ken Joncas (Walt)

Steve King (Turk)

Tommy Max (Candy)

Bree McKibbon (Judy)

Allan Meiusi (Fred)

Megan Roberts (Ingrid)

Shane Toland (Moose)

Nick Vradis (Shane)

THE GROWN-UPS

Lydia Chaban (Thelma the crossing guard)

Michelle Dionne (Mrs. Frost)

Charlotte Freedlander (Gayle — Noel and Lisa's stepmother)

Sari Friedland (Mrs. Brendakis, Degrassi Grocery owner)

Debra Hale (Auntie Lou)

Ralph Harrison (Cookie's dad)

Dave James (Duke — Griff's brother and guardian, also played Wheels' birth dad on *Degrassi Classic*)

Bruce Mackey (Mr. Mackey)

Gloria Manzl (Pete and Chuck's mom)

Alannah Myles (Cookie's mom)

R.D. Reid (Don Canard — Noel and Lisa's father)

Nancy Sinclair (Martin, Melanie, and Moose's mom, later Wheels' mom)

Edna Sternbach (Ida's mom)

Andy Stocks (Danny the crossing guard)

Wendy Watson (Mrs. Gonzales)

THE DEGRASSI CLASSIC ACTORS

Meet the actors who brought the characters of *Degrassi Junior High* and *Degrassi High* to life. There were a number of other young people who appeared on the show over the years, so if your friend's claim to fame is appearing on *Degrassi Classic* and you don't see the name here, it could still be true.

DAYO ADE
played Bryant Lister
"B.L.T." Thomas

Character's claim to fame: Dated Michelle; had trouble breaking up with Michelle

Now: Hollywood actor; has appeared in *The Shield*, *Joan of Arcadia*, *Alias*, and *Scrubs*

Along the way: Appeared in Canadian TV shows and movies such as *Top Cops*, *The Kids in the Hall*, *Rude*

Remembering: "Traveling to Yellowknife, [Northwest Territories], where I flew a plane, drummed at a drum dance, and rode in a dogsled.... When we started the show, I had no idea how big a deal it would be. *Degrassi* was my high school graduating class."

NINA ANNIS
played Lois

In real life: Actually lived on Degrassi Street (and still does)

Now: Trains performing dogs

FAQ: "People often come along Degrassi Street looking for the school, which, of course, isn't here. But I show them where Degrassi Grocery used to be. When I tell them I was on the show, they're always delighted."

DAVID ARMIN PARCELLS
played Claude Tanner

Character's claim to fame: Encouraged Caitlin to break the law; dramatically killed himself at school

Now: Wine buyer for a grocery chain in Detroit; records and performs electronica under the name Dai

The story behind the beard: His parents were away and he thought it would be fun to grow a beard. He auditioned with it, the producers liked it, and he was stuck with it — so he said at the time. But he still has it!

Remembering: "I remember just having a great time on set and off. It was, as a whole, a great experience."

SARA BALLINGALL
played Melanie Brodie

Character's claim to fame:
Kathleen's best friend; stole money from her mom to attend a concert with Snake

STEVE BEDERNJAK
played Clutch

Character's claim to fame:
Attracted to Lucy; drove the "splatter car"

Now: Freelance assistant editor for shows such as *Earth: Final Conflict*; married

Now it can be told: When Steve first had to pull the car up to the school and stop with a screech, he didn't actually have his driver's license yet.

MICHAEL BLAKE
played Paul

Character's claim to fame:
Clutch's best friend; Lucy's short-term boyfriend

Actor's claim to fame: Simba in *The Lion King* on stage in Toronto; has appeared in movies and TV series

Remembering: "I was only on the show for a short time, but I just remember feeling so comfortable and nurtured, especially in the workshops where they really worked to bring out our personalities."

KIRSTY BOURNE
played Tessa Campanelli

Character's claim to fame:
Discovered the fire in the junior high basement with Scooter; slept with Joey in *School's Out!*

Now: Teaches grade eight in Toronto; married

Nickname: "Doug. There were so many people with 'K' names that one day Darrin [Brown] got fed up and said, 'Just call her Doug.' And it stuck!"

DANAH-JEAN BROWN
played Trish

Character's claim to fame:
Wore her red hair in a spiky mohawk; a staff member on the *Degrassi (Junior High) Digest*

Actor's claim to fame: Also played Connie on *The Kids of Degrassi Street*

DARRIN BROWN
played Dwayne Myers

Character's claim to fame: Bullied Joey; became HIV-positive

Now: Second assistant director, mostly on U.S. feature films in Toronto, but also in Prague, Winnipeg, Calgary, and Boston

Along the way: Worked as a grip on televised NHL hockey games

Now it can be told: Afraid of needles, Darrin had an arm stand-in for the blood test shot in "Bad Blood, Part 2." That arm was really Neil Hope's.

CHRISTIAN CAMPBELL
played Todd

Character's claim to fame: Dale's best friend

Now: Writer, director, actor in New York City; played Bobby Warner on *All My Children*; has worked on numerous theatrical and film productions, some of which debuted at the Sundance Film Festival

Famous relative: His little sister Neve was not a repertory company member, but sometimes worked as an extra on *Degrassi High*.

MICHAEL CARRY
played Simon Dexter

Character's claim to fame: Worked as a model; was "murdered" in the shower scene of Lucy's movie

Now: Runs a film production company in Toronto

Remembering: "We filmed the shower scene in the dead of winter. There was no hot water in the basement where we filmed. To match the *Psycho* sequence somewhat, it took an entire day to film. I have never been so cold in my life!"

GEORGE CHAKER
played Nick

Character's claim to fame: Bullied Joey; was afraid of Dwayne after he was outed as being HIV-positive

Now: Owns Diesel Fitness, a boutique gym in Toronto; trains some celebrities

Remembering: "I went to Jarvis Collegiate, in the heart of the Toronto's gay district, and I was always worried that I would be recognized as the guy who made the homophobic remarks on *Degrassi* and they'd think I was really like that."

ANDY CHAMBERS
played Luke

Character's claim to fame: Provided the drugs that led to Shane's injury

Now: Props master for TV commercials in Vancouver; still takes acting classes and goes to auditions

Now it can be told: In order to audition, Andy forged the note that allowed him to skip class.

CHRISTOPHER CHARLESWORTH
played Scooter Webster

Character's claim to fame: Discovered the fire in the junior high basement with Tessa; was unsuccessful at raising sea monkeys with best friend Bartholemew

Actor's claim to fame: Was one of two who played older than he actually was; also played Benjamin on KDS

Now: Recruiter for a major Ontario university

SARAH CHARLESWORTH
played Susie Rivera

Character's claim to fame: Caitlin's best friend; Mr. Colby harassed her

Actor's claim to fame: Also played Casey on KDS

Sibling rivalry: Susie's little sister was played by Anais Granofsky's real little sister; fellow actor Christopher Charlesworth is Sarah's real little brother.

DANNY CIRACO
played Ricky

Character's claim to fame: Stage manager for the talent show

Now: Corporate and intellectual property lawyer in Toronto, working with Stephen Stohn

Remembering: "Some of us made up our own story lines. In one episode, an extra and I had a fist fight in the background. In another, Chrisa [Erodotou] and I staged a break-up scene — tears and all. Of course, these were all very subtle, but if you know to look for them, they're there."

AMANDA COOK
played Lorraine "L.D." Delacorte

Character's claim to fame: Afraid to visit her dad in hospital; had cancer, but beat it

Now: Freelance writer in South Africa; married, with two children

Remembering: "The absolute best moments were the ones in-between takes when all of us were silly and joking and just having fun. We were truly like a family and really enjoyed our time together."

IRENE COURAKOS
played Alexa Pappadopoulos

Character's claim to fame: Was given Stephanie's clothes; married Simon in *School's Out!*

Now: Teaches English as a Second Language at her Epikinoia School in Athens, Greece; married, with two daughters

Remembering: "I think of all the little things: Friday is Tie Day; boat bashes; going to the Gemini Awards that magical night; wading in the Georgia Strait [Vancouver] in the middle of winter; Anais jumping over a parking meter in Memphis."

TREVOR CUMMINGS
played Bartholemew Bond

Character's claim to fame:
Scooter's best friend; liked comic books

ANGELA DEISEACH
played Erica Farrell

Character's claim to fame: Had an abortion after a summer camp fling; went bowling in high heels

Now: Teaches Special Education part-time; teaches Spanish dance and other regional dance full-time

Remembering: "I've been on other sets and I've seen the kind of kissing-up that goes on. On *Degrassi*, you never needed to present a face or be on your guard. We weren't treated as commodities, but accepted for who we were."

MAUREEN DEISEACH
played Heather Farrell

Character's claim to fame: Kissed Wheels at her party; supported Erica, though she disagreed with her twin's abortion choice

Now: Teaches grade two in downtown Toronto

Along the way: Lots of travel

Remembering: "I mainly remember the day-to-day camaraderie and laughter."

SABRINA DIAS
played Jyoti

Character's claim to fame: Helped out when Caitlin had an epileptic seizure

Along the way: Earned a Bachelor's Degree in Engineering and a Master's Degree in Environmental

Studies; has worked as a color scientist and a ceramic engineer

Remembering: "Most of my memories are of off-camera times — hanging out with Colleen [Lam], Chrisa, and Karryn [Sheridan] in that library."

BYRD DICKENS
played Scott Smith

Character's claim to fame: Abused his girlfriend, Kathleen

In real life: Worked as a crew member (electric) on *Degrassi* when he wasn't acting

Now: Lives in Toronto; still works in the film industry doing

lighting for movies, TV shows, commercials, and music videos

Remembering: "I've been lucky enough to work and socialize with a few of the others from the show over the years, like Anais and Darrin [Brown]."

CRAIG DRISCOLL
played Rick Munro

Character's claim to fame: Abused by his father; Caitlin's first love interest

Now: Tattoo artist in Edmonton

Remembering: "I think that the one thing that stood out, and still does, is the recognition that you get. To this day, I still get recognized. I'm tattooing at Dragon FX in Edmonton and every day at the shop, someone comes in and asks me about *Degrassi*. The show had a huge impact on people and I got to be a small part of it."

CHRISA ERODOTOU
played Diana

Character's claim to fame: Got caught smoking; tried marijuana on her birthday with no effect other than an urge to eat the entire birthday cake

Now: Married, with a son; lives in Oshawa, Ontario

Remembering: "Sari [Friedland] taught me to smoke for the episode where my brother catches me. I had never tried it and I had to look convincing. But she threatened me with instant death if she ever caught me doing it for real."

MARSHA FERGUSON
played Cindy

Character's claim to fame: Stole B.L.T. from Michelle; outspoken member of the girls' volleyball team

In real life: Marsha won medals for body-building as a teenager.

CAMERON GRAHAM
played Dale

Character's claim to fame: Lucy's rival for sports time and student council office; one of the "Dancing Jockettes" in the talent show

Actor's claim to fame: Leading role on *Paradise Falls*; various roles on commercials, television, and films

Now: Still acting, and branching into writing

ANAIS GRANOFSKY
played Lucy Fernandez

Character's claim to fame: Videotaped everything; injured in a car accident in *School's Out!*

Now: A filmmaker in Toronto

Along the way: Graduated from New York University and received the top prize at the Tisch School of the Arts

REBECCA HAINES
played Kathleen Mead

Character's claim to fame: Anorexic; had an alcoholic mom; abused by her boyfriend

Now: Works in child mental health research and part-time on her Ph.D. in Public Health Sciences

Remembering: "I have been able to visit with quite a few young people who are critically ill. Just to see that look of surprise when they see me come into the hospital room — that is something that is irreplaceable."

SARA HOLMES
played Alison

Character's claim to fame: Rescued from drowning by Snake in *School's Out!*; came between Caitlin and her boyfriend in the kick-off reunion special of *TNG*

Now: Teaches high school drama in Markham, Ontario

Now it can be told: "I would have done it whether they were paying me or not!"

NEIL HOPE
played Derek "Wheels" Wheeler

Character's claim to fame: Parents killed by a drunk driver; drove drunk and killed a child in *School's Out!*

Actor's claim to fame: Also played Griff on *KDS*

JACY HUNTER
played Amy Holmes

Character's claim to fame: Traded clothes with Alison in the girls' washroom during an argument; vied with Alison for Snake

Now: Teaches grades seven and eight in London, Ontario

Now it can be told: That was Jacy's behind you saw every week in the opening credits.

JOHN IOANNOU
played Alex Yankou

Character's claim to fame: Stayed up all night to finish an essay; had trouble kissing Tessa

Actor's claim to fame: Also played Pete on *KDS*

Now it can be told: Carl Langschmidt remembers that filming a scene once took so long they had to shave John's five o'clock shadow to preserve continuity.

DEAN IFILL
played Bronco Davis

Character's claim to fame: Student president at Degrassi High; Lucy's boyfriend

Now: Produces films; runs the Act Out project, which helps at-risk youth get their lives on track through the arts

Now it can be told: On a publicity trip to Halifax, he decided to slip away and check out some of the nightlife, and the Mounties had to be sent to find him.

ANDY JEKABSONS
played Mark

Character's claim to fame: Played more background Frisbee than anyone else; after Wheels' parents' death, when the teacher said that the students would want to share their pain, he piped up, "I don't wanna share any pain!"

Now: A focus puller in Toronto

Along the way: Worked on the camera crews of many commercials, Canadian TV shows, and American productions

MICHELLE JOHNSON-MURRAY
played Tabi

Character's claim to fame: Terrorized Melanie and Kathleen in the hairspray corridor; danced with Dwayne at the last dance

Now: A psychotherapist in Thorold, Ontario; has a daughter

Now it can be told: Lied about her address so she would be eligible to audition (actors had to live inside the Greater Toronto Area to be considered)

SAMER KAMAL
played Mack

Character's claim to fame: Praised Caitlin's editorial supporting Spike

Now it can be told: Famous among the cast as the host of probably the wildest party they ever had!

ANNA KEENAN
played Rainbow

Character's claim to fame: Often wore a beret

In real life: She's Cathy Keenan's sister.

Now: A photographer specializing in photography for musicians and artists; also works as an assistant production manager for the same animation company as her sister

CATHY KEENAN
played Liz O'Rourke

Character's claim to fame: Spike's best friend; sexually abused as a child

Now: A production coordinator at an animation studio in Toronto

Along the way: Still close friends with Amanda Stepto

Remembering: "People watch the reruns and think of you as famous. It's tough because you're just working at your regular job."

NIKI KEMENY
played Voula

Character's claim to fame: Made the speech when Stephanie was too drunk; picked up for shoplifting with Lucy

Now: Teaches English at Conestoga College in Guelph, Ontario

Remembering: "I just remember the great atmosphere, hanging out on and off camera, sitting in the library, doing crafts together."

COLLEEN LAM
played Vivian

Character's claim to fame: Often costumed as a cheerleader; won second place in the Degrassi Science Fair

Now: Provides child care and volunteers for charity

Along the way: Graduated in TV/Radio Broadcasting; interned at *Canada AM*, *CTV News*, CHUM FM/AM Radio, and has worked in British Columbia and Thunder Bay, Ontario

CARL LANGSCHMIDT
played David

Character's claim to fame: Was a member of the cheerleading squad

Now: Provides technical support for the computer network at the Royal Ontario Museum

Remembering: "For a kid at that age, it was a great job. I got to work among people who got along, got fed amazing food, and spent the whole day acting out school — with no homework!"

KYRA LEVY
played Maya Goldberg

Character's claim to fame: Left out of a trip to the movies by her friends because of her wheelchair

Now: Her band, Psychokey, has released five albums; co-owns a recording studio with her husband in St. Lucia

FAQ: Kyra does have a disability that requires the use of leg braces. The wheelchair was used on the show so that Kyra could perform sitting down, which was easier on her.

ANDREW LOCKIE
played Casey

Character's claim to fame: Spokesman for Classroom 9B; challenged Arthur's class in the UNICEF drive

Now: Married, with a son

Along the way: Has been an outdoor education coordinator in New Zealand and traveled to Australia, Fiji, and the Cook Islands

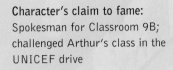

ARLENE LOTT
played Nancy Kramer

Character's claim to fame: Editor of the *Degrassi (Junior High) Digest;* student council vice president

Actor's claim to fame: Also played Rachel, class rep and yearbook editor, on KDS

Now: Has done design work for Epitome Pictures, and created the artwork for the sign at Bruce Mackey Park

MAUREEN McKAY
played Michelle Accette

Character's claim to fame: B.L.T.'s girlfriend; moved out on her own at sixteen

Now: Corporate and commercial lawyer in Toronto; married, with a son and daughter

Along the way: Bought a house in Greece, which she and her family visit each year

Remembering: "My entire life would have been different if there hadn't been *Degrassi.*"

BILL PARROTT
played Shane McKay

Character's claim to fame: Fathered Spike's baby; took acid at a concert and fell off a bridge, sustaining permanent brain damage

Actor's claim to fame: Was the first to call Amanda Stepto "Spike"

Now: An actor in Toronto; has appeared in commercials and in films such as *Evil Dead*

SILUCK SAYSANASY
played Yick Yu

Character's claim to fame: Arthur's best friend — the brave one of the two; kissed Yankou's girlfriend, Tessa

Now: An assistant director in Toronto

Along the way: Has maintained a close friendship with Pat Mastroianni; worked as a kid-wrangler on TNG

KARRYN SHERIDAN
played Vicky

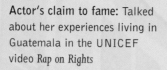

Actor's claim to fame: Talked about her experiences living in Guatemala in the UNICEF video *Rap on Rights*

Now: Teaches drama in Vancouver; married, with a daughter

Remembering: "Michelle Goodeve brushed off setbacks as nothing. She taught me that a confident woman didn't let little things get to her. She was a positive, upbeat mentor to me."

NICOLE STOFFMAN
played Stephanie Kaye

Character's claim to fame: Ran for student council president on a campaign of kissing the boys; changed into trashy clothes when she got to school

Now: Performs with her band, Le Jazz Boheme, based in Toronto

Along the way: Left *Degrassi* for a leading role in the Canadian sitcom *Learning the Ropes*; eventually decided that acting and the film and television world were not for her, and took up singing

VINCENT WALSH
played Patrick

Character's claim to fame: Wrote a song for Spike; had an Irish accent

Actor's claim to fame: Leading roles in Canadian, Irish, and American film, television, and

stage, such as *Shattered City: The Halifax Explosion, Hemingway vs. Callaghan,* and *Saving Private Ryan*

ANNABELLE WAUGH
played Dorothy

Character's claim to fame: Played Arthur's cousin; patched up Yick and Arthur's feud at Christmas

In real life: Duncan Waugh's sister

Now: A recipe developer for *Canadian Living* and *Homemakers* magazines

DUNCAN WAUGH
played Arthur Kobalewsky

Character's claim to fame: Broke Yick's "Ming" vase; his mother won a major lottery prize

Now: No one knows for sure. Some say he wanders the earth helping those in need. Others say

no, that was David Carradine from the *Kung Fu* TV series. Either way, we're pretty sure his head is shaved!

KEITH WHITE
played Tim

Character's claim to fame: Good at magic; took Liz to see The Pogues

In real life: Wrote the song that was The Savages' hit on *Degrassi*

LISA WILLIAMS
played Joy

Character's claim to fame: Predicted Claude would go to hell because suicide is a sin

Actor's claim to fame: Was on *KDS* as an extra

Now: Married, with a daughter and twin sons; lives in Brampton, Ontario

That Special Teacher

MICHELLE GOODEVE
played Ms. Karen Avery

Character's claim to fame: Was the object of Caitlin's odd dreams; left Degrassi for Rainbow Valley

Now: Co-creator, co-writer, and co-producer of *Barnstormers*, a documentary series for The Outdoor Life Network. Stars in — and flies an antique biplane on — the show

The Characters & Cast of
DEGRASSI: THE NEXT GENERATION

It's the same neighborhood and there are several familiar faces, but there's a new generation of kids dealing with the trials and tribulations of growing up at Degrassi Community School. Meet the actors whose characters crossed over to the new show. Get to know the young cast and their TV counterparts, as well as some of the actors who play their teachers and parents.

JOEY JEREMIAH
Played by Pat Mastroianni

ON BEING JOEY

I know what this show means to Canada and for Canadian television. To be part of that, for me — so high-profile in the original series — I'm so honored to be "that guy."

ON SELLING HIS HATS FOR CANCER RESEARCH

I've sold all the old hats; all but one. My mom has it forever and I won't touch it. I have the one from the new series that I wore in the reunion special, and that's sitting on my Gemini. I have no clue where the old red ones went. And my Firefly skateboard. They borrowed my skateboard for foley and never gave it back. Someone offered me $1,000 US for my *Degrassi Junior High* jacket. I said, "No! It means too much to me." I'll never wear it, but it means that much to me. I want my kid to have it one day.

ON THE TIME BETWEEN DEGRASSIs

In between was *Liberty Street*, and I hosted *Music Works* — and we've just had the tenth anniversary of that show. I went to L.A. for four years and it was kind of an awakening experience. I met some great people and made some good friends. My "university years" were spent in L.A., and I spent just about as much as a university student would have! Can you believe I couldn't get a job as a movie usher in Hollywood? I went in because I needed some money, said I'd do anything, and the guy wouldn't hire me! I couldn't help thinking, "Dude! If you knew who I was in my home and native land!"

ON COMING BACK

I was happy to hand the torch off to the new cast back in 2001. The old characters were originally just going to be there for the one episode. I was very envious during the reunion special because I knew what was ahead for the new cast. I was looking at them, seeing myself, and thinking, "They're so green, they're so young, they're so wide-eyed, and darn, I'm not going to be part of that." Then they expanded the role, and I thought, "Here's a chance to relive my youth, correct some of the mistakes I made early on, and hopefully show to myself and to my peers that I have improved and bring something to the show that the fans want to see, and in all honesty, get some financial security!"

ON THE BEST PART

I used to say to [my wife] Carmela, "I wish you knew me then, when there was excitement and parties and awards. We could have had so much fun back in those days together," and now we get to do that together.

Junior high: manages Stephanie's campaign • starts The Zit Remedy • repeats a grade • attends final dance with Caitlin **High school:** gets bullied by Dwayne • gets dumped by Caitlin • gets more help from Caitlin • attends final dance with Caitlin • proposes to Caitlin • breaks up with Caitlin **While we weren't watching:** marries Julia • opens a car dealership • becomes a father to Angela • becomes a widower **Now that we're watching:** takes in late wife's son Craig • dates Sydney • gets Caitlin back; she moves in • accepts Caitlin's proposal • breaks up with Caitlin — for good?

CAITLIN RYAN
Played by Stacie Mistysyn

ON HOW SHE GOT ON THE KIDS OF DEGRASSI STREET

I was taking dance classes and a flyer was delivered that said, "Kids Wanted." I showed the paper to my parents, who luckily allowed me to go and audition. For the audition, I was wearing a tank top, shorts, and flip-flops. I didn't know what to wear to an audition! But it probably worked to my advantage because they were looking for kids just being kids.

ON THE EARLY DAYS

The first few seasons of *Degrassi Junior High* were chaotic because there were so many of us. We were supposed to be getting tutored, but we were very rowdy. Laura Papsin was our tutor. Stefan [Brogren] would always be making me laugh so hard and so loud, and she was always shushing me, trying to distract me away from Stefan with some activity like rug-hooking. I think I had a bit of a crush on Stefan back then. I'd always be playing lame practical jokes on him, like tying his shoelaces together while he was sleeping.

ON MOVING TO LOS ANGELES

I decided to go for three months and if I didn't like it, I would come back. I'd always been afraid and curious to go to L.A. It's the mecca for the entertainment industry and I was actually born there. Having my agent go out there and take me under her wing was the invitation I needed. I landed a guest spot and was able to buy a used car. [Repco colleague] Bill Parrott came to L.A. with me (as a friend!) with the understanding that he'd teach me to drive and share rent. When I went for my test, the examiner was actually laughing at my car. L.A. was a whole crazy other world that was fascinating and horrible all at the same time. I realized that as much as I had kept trying to escape acting, I kept going back.

ON SCHOOL'S OUT!

It was amazing because I remember Pat and I got to sit down with Yan [Moore] and brainstorm. We talked about a lot of the plot and what would work. He was always really good about listening to us, and I felt like we had a lot of input into that story.

ON BEING ON THE NEW SHOW

I love being part of such a great show. I love how my character is ever-evolving. She's still trying to find herself and figure things out. That's what makes her interesting. She's not a perfect person; she has a glam side and a dorky/awkward side. She'll always be dear to my heart, that Caitlin.

Junior high: dances with Joey • tutors Joey • attends dance with Joey **High school:** dumps Joey • helps Joey face up to his learning disability • goes to semi-formal with Joey • graduates a year early • loses virginity to Joey • discovers he's been sleeping with Tessa all summer • dumps Joey **While we weren't watching:** makes a TV career as a crusading environmentalist on *Ryan's Planet* **Now that we're watching:** returns from L.A. for high-school reunion • moves to Toronto • gets together with Joey again • buys Joey's house and moves in with him • proposes to Joey • moves away, breaking Joey's heart

CHRISTINE "SPIKE" NELSON
Played by Amanda Stepto

ON BEING AN ICON

It was a combination of the hair and the pregnancy. There weren't a lot of pregnant teen characters on TV, and I got a lot of mail from young women in the same situation who seemed to appreciate the way the story line was tackled.

ON THE HAIR

I auditioned with my hair like that because that was the way I wore my hair in real life. Final Net was the strongest hairspray of the day, so lots of Final Net — it was also pretty cheap.

ON WHETHER SHE WAS LIKE SPIKE

Looks, yes. Character, I think a little bit. We [actors] were pretty much ourselves on screen and that's what made it a bit more realistic. Sometimes [Spike and I] had different story lines, like being pregnant. If I took that out of Spike, I think we were pretty similar. For example, Spike is for animal rights and that's the way I am. When she was looking for a part-time job and was made fun of by the diner owner — that happened all the time in real life because of my hair.

ON HER FIRST KISSING SCENE

That one scene of kissing just seemed to take forever. I can remember Kit saying, "Okay, now make more noise!" I was absolutely horrified! All I was thinking was, "Say 'cut.' Say 'cut.' Please say 'cut.'"

ON LIFE AFTER DEGRASSI HIGH

I pursued acting, but it was hard trying to break free of the Spike image. I graduated with an honors B.A. in Political Science and History, but I love to travel! I was a full-time university student, but I also had a full-time job at a store in Kensington Market [in Toronto] that imported from Mexico, India, Thailand, Indonesia, and other places. I went on buying trips and that made me want to travel more. As soon as I graduated, I moved to Japan for a year, which was an awesome experience.

ON SPIKE THE GROWN-UP

I find her boring, considering what she was like as a teenager. She's still fashionable, which is good, but she makes these yuppie dinners all the time. She still looks a little like me. I have input into the clothes she wears. I go with Canadian designers who are a little bit funky.

ON THE NEW SHOW

My character has become a bit dull. I have to tell myself that the focus of the show is the younger cast and you're a supporting character, there to help the main characters do what they have to do. But at the same time, you're coming from a past where you did have a big part and now you have a small part, and you have to put that in focus. I have so much fun when I'm there. When Stefan and I are doing a scene, we're usually trying to make each other laugh and ruin the other's close-ups. When Stacie and I have a scene together, we just have a blast on set.

Junior high: has sex with Shane; gets pregnant • worries she will flunk • gives birth to Emma **High school:** is a single mom • dates Patrick • asks Snake to semi-formal **While we weren't watching:** raises Emma • takes over mom's hair salon **Now that we're watching:** marries Snake • has second child (Jack) • deals with Emma's teen years

MR. ARCHIE "SNAKE" SIMPSON
Played by Stefan Brogren

ON REVISITING SNAKE

You really just have to trust the writers; that whatever they're going to do with Snake ten years later is going to fit into the whole stream of things. They could do whatever they want because ten years have passed and people change so much. They really could have made him a monster. And then we'd just have to roll with it if that were the case.

ON SNAKE MATURING

I just figured I would always be known to the viewers as Snake, and I am. I'm used to having people yell, "Snake!" at me on the street. But then I was at a climbing gym during the first season of TNG and there were a lot of kids around. They came up and said, "Mr. Simpson?" It marked a weird transition for me from child to adult.

ON A PROMISE MADE

When I first started this show [TNG], I made a promise to myself that I wasn't going to be the pompous older actor to the younger kids. I was going to work with these kids, so I had to talk to them like full-on adults and play with them. So from right off the top, I had a really good relationship with them, the same sort of relationship that I had on the old show. When we're on set, they'll tell me a secret in the same way they would tell each other.

ON YOUNG SNAKE

Snake was one of the most insecure kids on the old show. It would work like this: Joey would say, "Come on, let's steal your parents' car," and Snake would say, "No, that's a bad idea." Joey would say, "Come on, let's do it!" Snake would say, "OK." By the time we got to *School's Out!*, all the characters said, "I'm not going to take it any more. I'm not a kid any more." That was the first time Snake really switched over into, "I'm an adult."

ON WHY DEGRASSI IS DIFFERENT

Spinner is a hero, but I don't think there are many shows on television where you would show one of your lead characters writing "faggot" on the bathroom wall about one of his best friends. Manny, who was one of the sweetest characters at the beginning of the series, took a total turn, and people do that. On *Beverly Hills, 90210*, Brandon was never the one with the problem. He was the one who knew the kid with the problem. On this show, you can have your main kids really make mistakes, and it changes the characters completely and they have to go down a different route. They don't end up exactly where they started, like on sitcoms. Emma's now changed, and subsequently Snake and Spike are changed.

ON VIEWER REACTION TO THE CANCER STORY LINE

Halfway through the season's airing, I got a lot of people coming up to me, very concerned that Simpson was going to die. A woman approached me and said, "So is he better? Is he still ill?" I said, "I think he's in remission, I think he's good." And she went as far as to say, "Are you OK?" I had to tell her, "I'm fine! It's just the character."

Junior high: forms The Zit Remedy • gets into trouble with Joey and Wheels • invites Melanie on a date • listens as brother reveals he is gay **High school:** discovers Claude's body • tells Michelle he likes her **While we weren't watching:** earns a teaching degree • gets a job teaching media and computer skills at Degrassi Community School **Now that we're watching:** marries Spike • becomes Emma's stepfather • becomes a dad to baby Jack • learns he has cancer • undergoes chemotherapy • helps students deal with the school shooting

MR. DAN RADITCH
Played by Dan Woods

ON BECOMING MR. RADITCH

I was about two weeks away from quitting acting — I'd applied for a job as a
school caretaker when I was called for the audition. I'd also applied to work on
air at a radio station. Then, in the same week, I got the part and the radio station
offered me the job. I was lucky to be able to combine them. It was my first
regular gig, yet I was the oldest, most veteran guy in the cast. The kids would
come to me for acting advice.

ON MR. RADITCH

"Yuppie" was the buzzword at the time, and I figured Raditch was one — once the
bell rang, he jumped in his car and went to sip cappuccino. I don't know if he's
married or single, straight or gay. The directors and I never played it
either way. There are clues about Mr. Raditch's outside life. We
see his house in *Degrassi High*. There are little die-cast cars in boxes
to decorate his office. There's a picture on the desk of me with a
fishing buddy — or gay partner? I never wear a wedding ring,
and I was good friends with Ms. Avery — or were we dating?

ON HIS FAVORITE EPISODES

My favorite moment on the classic series was telling Joey he is
being held back. It was challenging to be caring and sincere with
a character Raditch hadn't been overtly caring toward before.
The episode where Raditch lost the exam was fun, a bit madcap.
For example, there was a speeding ticket on top of the papers
he has when he gets back to the classroom. On *The Next
Generation*, I loved doing "Take on Me," the *Breakfast Club*
tribute. On breaks while everyone else took it easy, I'd be in
my van, watching the teacher on the DVD, trying to get
that swagger just right.

ON HIS CAR SHOW

I've had a few incarnations of my car show. A partner and I made the pilot of *Classic Car Restorations* with borrowed equipment and took it to the Speedvision network in the United States. Then we got into real trouble because they said, "Go ahead and do it." A few financial adjustments later, it is back as *Chop, Cut, Rebuild,* and I'm now a full-time producer in California where I live with my wife and three kids.

ON THE DEMISE OF MR. RADITCH

With the car show doing so well in California, it was difficult for me to be popping in and out of Toronto to do TNG. The writers found a reason to have me "transferred": the school shooting. Linda [Schuyler] was phenomenally gracious about letting me move forward as a producer. But if they need me again for a Raditch appearance, I'd do it in a heartbeat.

Junior high years: says, "Greetings scholars" for the first time **High school years:** becomes vice-principal of Degrassi High **Community School years:** becomes principal • hires Archie "Snake" Simpson • is reassigned to another school after the shooting

LIBERTY VAN ZANDT
Played by Sarah Barrable-Tishauer

born july 6, 1988

Liberty is the boss of her grade. She's super-organized, committed, and motivated — if something gets done, Liberty's behind it. Of course, that doesn't mean it always goes exactly according to plan! What the rest of Degrassi doesn't know about is her tender side. Only we viewers know how long she's harbored that crush on J.T. that's finally becoming a genuine relationship.

ON HER START

I've always been around the theater — my whole family is involved in the arts, and my parents founded a professional theater company. So when I saw an open casting call for the stage version of *The Lion King*, I auditioned. I was given a callback slip, but when no one followed up, I was so disappointed. Then, about three months later, they put the call out again, and I tried again. After four callbacks, learning several song and dance numbers, the casting director called and offered me the part of Young Nala. I was ecstatic! I performed in the role for nine months — the standard changeover for young cast members — at the Princess of Wales Theatre — the same stage where Jake Goldsbie and Jake Epstein started out. After that, I got an agent and was cast in a principal role in the made-for-TV movie *Red Sneakers*, with the late Gregory Hines. I then auditioned for *Degrassi*.

ON WHY SHE LOVES DEGRASSI

I love that *Degrassi* is a Canadian show and is good enough to be broadcast all over the world. Not enough attention is paid to Canadian film and television, so it's great when Canadian drama is received with the same excitement as shows that come from the U.S. *Degrassi* is reaching an audience that's not often tapped into, and we deal with heavier issues than most shows. *Degrassi* is also lucky to have an amazing group of people who work on the show. From the producers right through, everyone really believes in what we're doing.

ON HER FREE TIME

I basically just do what normal kids do — shopping, movies, hanging out with friends. I also do a lot of volunteer work. At school, I've helped found a committee for student-driven volunteer initiatives. We work in association with a government program called Empowered Student Partnerships and have been able to carry through with some amazing campaigns. A fundraising campaign that I started is called the Toronto Schools Snowsuit Challenge. We're challenging schools to raise money that will be used to buy new snowsuits for children in need.

ON DINNERTIME

The rest of my free time is taken up with cooking. I love to cook, and seeing my friends' faces when I serve them a special meal is truly priceless. I've learned Chinese and Italian techniques from a friend of mine who is a chef. I've now become the cook for my family. I go to the local markets to pick up fresh ingredients and create my own recipes for dinner parties — I think my mom's fairly relieved about that!

ON HER FUTURE

I definitely want to continue to act; it's my dream to be on Broadway. I'd like to stay in show business if I can, but I can see myself going into the business end of things. I will be going to university in a couple years and would like to get an M.B.A. Linda has said to me that she could see me as a producer. I'm also interested in sales, advertising, and marketing, so I'll just have to wait and see what comes my way.

SEAN CAMERON
Played by **Daniel Clark**
born october 14, 1985

Sean was sent away to live with his brother, Tracker, in Toronto because he broke a boy's eardrum in a fight. When Tracker moved to Alberta, Sean had to manage on his own. It's been a rough experience for him and he's taken some wrong turns, like stealing Mr. Simpson's computer, and some right ones, like making it up to him by fixing his car. He put his life on the line when Rick aimed his gun at Emma. Injured and deeply frightened after the shooting incident, Sean finally returned home to his parents in Wasaga Beach.

ON HIS RÉSUMÉ

I started out on stage in *Beauty and the Beast* and I had roles in *Eerie, Indiana; I Was a Sixth Grade Alien; Goosebumps;* and a variety of movies, including *Earth: Final Conflict*. It wasn't strange to me to come on to a show that had a history because *Eerie, Indiana* was also a revival. But I was really excited to get the role on *Degrassi* because I knew it would deal with relevant, real-life issues.

ON LEAVING DEGRASSI

I had an awesome time on *Degrassi* and I would come back if there was a significant reason to — it would have to mean something. But I'm an American and I had to be in the U.S. for the 2004 election. I've become very politically active, though I'm neither a Republican nor a Democrat. I'm also getting my real estate license and taking a Bachelor's Degree in Business and Marketing to keep my options open.

ON CARS

I love cars — muscle cars. I have a Camaro V8 that I got on eBay and I rebuilt. I did a good job — it's not "chopped" at all. I'm pretty good at mechanics; I know what I'm doing. A car is a work of art. People *design* cars — everything you do to a car has to match. I also have a Honda Prelude that's a show car. I just finished it and I plan to enter it in shows this year. I like a well-rounded vehicle that doesn't just have nice rims. You've got to work on the motor, the brakes, and the interior has to match — you can't go overboard on just one part of a car. I've been interested in cars since I was two. My grandpa would ask, "Daniel, what kind of car is that?" And I'd say "Chevy" or "Toyota" or whatever it was.

ON TRAVEL

I was born in Chicago, grew up in Florida. I've been all over North America, and every place is different — the air, the people, the culture. Road trips are nice. I take them a lot. You *have* to travel across the U.S on the interstate in a great car — or any car! — at least once in your life. You get to see all of the U.S. through your car window. You're

driving through the mountains of Colorado and if they're freshly dusted with snow they're really nice to look at. I did it once straight through in forty-four hours from L.A. to Toronto. If I had gotten tired, I would have pulled over, but I didn't! I would have gotten there quicker, but there was a storm near Chicago.

ON HOW TO MAKE CHEESECAKE

I make probably the best cheesecake. The trick is you have to watch it when it's baking. Some cheesecakes you just put in the fridge, but I think you have to bake it. It's all in the timing. You have to get it when it's just ready, not overcooked. The other thing is too many people put too much sugar in the topping. Just chop up the strawberries; maybe put a *little* sugar in. You don't even need to. Good fresh strawberries are sweet on their own.

PAIGE MICHALCHUK
Played by Lauren Collins
born august 29, 1986

Paige is the cool one, the cheerleader, the Alpha she-wolf of her pack. And when she said, "Jump," Spinner said, "How high?" But sometimes Paige gets what she doesn't want, and when she was raped at a party, her life fell apart. To make matters worse, when she took the rapist to court, he was acquitted. A new relationship with student teacher Mr. Oleander may ease some of the pain. Or it may bring pain anew.

ON BEING DISCOVERED

I started in community theater when I was about ten, and the woman who ran the company was an agent. After the show closed, she said, "What would you think about doing something more professional?" and I said, "Sure!" The first thing I ever did was an ABC-TV movie. I played Susan Lucci's daughter. It was a great way to start.

ON PLAYING THE "MEAN GIRL"

The monologue for my audition was hilarious! Up until then I'd always played the nice girl, the sweet girl, the girl next door. Finally, I got this really mean role. That was cool. Paige is the most fun character I've played.

She's not that typical mean girl. She's gone through a lot — the rape story line. That would affect anyone greatly and even a strong person like Paige it would hit hard, and it has. The writers have done an amazing job showing her progression.

ON WHAT TRIPS HER UP

I'm pretty klutzy. If you know me, you know I'm always in running shoes or flip flops. [The writers] always make me run in heels, so I'm always falling over. Oh, and cheerleading, that's another thing I hate doing! In the episode where Paige breaks her leg, that was one of the most embarrassing things I've ever had to film.

They used a stunt person, but they had to show me hitting the ground and screaming. I was supposed to be falling from eight feet in the air, but they had me falling from a box that was one foot off the ground. The day they filmed it, people said, "That was *so* funny!" and I was thinking, "What does that mean? Is that good, or is it really bad?"

ON HEATHER SINCLAIR

Paige and Heather seem to have some beef. It would be interesting to find out someday what the problem is.

ON ON-SCREEN KISSING

During the rape scene I was scared. Shawn Roberts [Dean] was much older than me. He was nineteen or twenty at the time and I was fifteen, but I've grown up. I realize that it's part of the job, what they pay you to do.

ON THE "GLAMOUR"

There are many challenges. Even the little things — so many changes, early morning call times, being on location, and long hours. It kind of bothers me when people say it's such a glamorous job, because it's really not; there's more to it. But someone's got to do it! [Long laugh.]

ON THE EVENTUAL END OF DEGRASSI

We never know for sure if the show's going to come back, but someday, it will be the last season. There'll be a piece of me that's missing. And then there's Paige. I heard Jason Priestley say once in an interview that he felt like he'd made a new friend [of his character on 90210]. It sounds silly, but that's totally how I feel about Paige. It would — well — be like she died.

ON WHETHER SHE WOULD GAIN WEIGHT FOR A ROLE, AS RENÉE ZELLWEGER DID IN BRIDGET JONES'S DIARY

Yeah, I think I would. I don't think it's necessarily...healthy, but I think that it's great that a leading woman of her stature in the business didn't mind doing it. I think there are many people at her level who would never do it because they wouldn't want to be seen with a less-than-perfect figure. So I've got to really respect her for that.

JAMES TIBERIUS "J.T." YORKE
Played by Ryan Cooley

born may 18, 1988

J.T. and Toby started grade seven as inseparable best buddies, but their relationship has not always gone smoothly. J.T. is growing up a little faster in some ways than his pal — his interest in girls far outstrips Toby's passion for Dungeons & Dragons. He's also taking on leadership roles at school — directing the play written by his serious new girlfriend, Liberty.

ON HOW HE WOULD LIKE TO SEE J.T. DEVELOP

Maybe do something new in the Liberty story line — massive fight, a break up, or continue and get deeper into that — something a little different that nobody's expecting because it's been leading up to that. He's been changing his friends, going out with Liberty. I'm always happy with what the writers come up with — I'm always looking for the challenge. They find it, and then I work with it.

ON ACTING AS A CAREER

It's absolutely what I want to do. I've been doing it since I was nine and at one point I had the lead role in I Was a Sixth-Grade Alien. I want to try and be as successful as I can possibly be. The shows I've done while growing up, I hope will be the stepping stone to a successful career as an adult actor.

ON SUCCESS

I would like to be happy with my own success. I'm not looking for immense fame, but for my satisfaction and the respect of others. I'm doing lots of theater stuff in my high school, and I'd like to explore more of that side. I would also like to get into the movie side. It'd be cool to go to L.A. and get "the big one." I'm doing all the auditions I can and keeping all my options open and I'll see where it will take me.

ON ALTERNATIVES

This industry can be rough. So I definitely want to go to university, get my B.F.A. in Drama. If my acting doesn't work out, I would love to teach English and Drama in high school. I think I would enjoy that just as much, but I'll stick with *Degrassi* for as long as it lasts, I hope.

ON NEW OPPORTUNITIES

I've had the experience of doing media interviews and getting to go to the Gemini Awards. I've been given the opportunity to travel and interact with fans. Los Angeles was incredible. Two thousand kids showed up at this mall — mainly screaming girls. We were ushered through by security and fans would jump out through the clothes racks just to see or touch us, banging on elevator doors. It's fun, but it's crazy.

ON WRITING

I like to write stories. I tend to go on and explain myself too much. My teacher got a story of mine published in a magazine. It was sort of speculative fiction. It was about a world war and nuclear weapons. In it, the president gets captured — and the U.S. keeps bombing the enemy and he gets killed because of the bombs. A little twist.

ON WHEN HE GROWS UP

I'll starve to death. I can't cook! I'll just have to live near a Pizza Pizza. Honestly, I once set a stove on fire trying to make Kraft Dinner! Actually, I'm not too bad at the Michelina's things — you know, you peel back the plastic wrap and put it in the microwave?

RICK MURRAY

Played by Ephraim Ellis

born february 23, 1985

Everyone at Degrassi hated Rick. As soon as he started dating Terri, Ashley was suspicious of him. And even after they broke up, he pursued Terri, finally pushing her once too hard and putting her into a coma. Ostracized and bullied by nearly everyone, Rick snapped and brought a gun to school. He shot Jimmy and would have shot Emma, if not for Sean's intervention. Rick's death had an impact on everyone.

ON WHY HE LOVES ACTING

I want to be what I have seen in the movies I have loved, to tell stories and affect other people in the same ways. I wish I could affect an audience in the way that this actor, this director, this writer are affecting me when I watch a movie or show. The idea of storytelling has always been fascinating to me. I've always had a big interest in history and myth and stuff like that. It's neat to see how people sitting around the campfire telling stories and sharing myths has evolved into this kind of new art form, television and film, that we see today.

ON GETTING INSIDE A BAD CHARACTER'S HEAD

What's really challenging is trying to find something within that character that you can identify with, actually love and enjoy about that character, and therefore use that as a doorway through which all the rest of it comes out. The only two things I share with Rick — I'm a huge theater nerd and I am probably going to be a hopeless romantic for the rest of my life. Everything else — not me!

ON HIS CHARACTER BEING KILLED OFF

I wasn't disappointed at all, because after the third season, Rick's story line had ended, when he pushed Terri into the rock and kind of fled for the border. I thought I was done, so when I got the call that I was being brought back, I thought, "*Why?* What can they do?" Linda brought me in, sat me down, and we had this little discussion about where the character was going. She asked, "Do you have any idea what's going on?" and I said, "I don't...know...do I kill someone? Does someone die?" And she said, "Sort of."

ON THE PAINT-COVERED SUIT

It was *great* on screen, absolutely fantastic and I'm so happy that Stefan [Scaini, Director] said "no" to me when I said Rick could have taken a shower when he got home, because it was ridiculously uncomfortable. I was not having a good time wandering around in the paint. But I am so happy that it was decided to keep me in the paint for most of the time, because it added so much to the sadness of this kid coming back to the school and not even cleaning himself up after this disgusting act of humiliation.

ON A CERTAIN PROP

In the kissing contest episode, the prize was a set of dice — Dungeons and Dragons dice. We're on set and Jake Goldsbie is sitting there holding the prop saying, "I have no freaking idea what these are used for. What is this?" And I just answered, "Yeah, no idea," then kind of hid my face because...I was aware of what they were used for.

ON HIS FAVORITE MOVIE

It's one of the funniest movies ever made. The comedic timing in the very first *Star Wars* is spot on! Every single joke in that movie comes at exactly the right time. And I know that's not what the main focus of the film is, but when you have the secondary characteristic of a film that is so perfect and has so much attention and care put into it, it's kind of neat.

CRAIG MANNING
Played by Jake Epstein
born january 16, 1987

Craig is the half-brother of young Angela, Joey Jeremiah's daughter. His father abused him and Joey gave him a home. He's had a confusing time growing up, feeling too strongly for two girls and a potential baby, feeling nothing after his father's sudden death, and feeling too hurt when Ashley said no to marriage. It all adds up to bipolar disorder, a condition he must learn to deal with for the rest of his life.

ON CRAIG

When I first got the script for Craig, I was really intrigued because he was very smart in a way and I really related to him. He's the most problem-plagued character on the show. More bad things have happened to him than anyone else. His mother died of cancer, his father's abusive. Then, his father dies, then he goes and he moves in with Joey, then he's cheating on girls, then he becomes bipolar, runs away...

ON WHY HE LOVES ACTING

I get to be someone other than myself — [laughs] not that I don't like myself or anything! It's a game, it's this little game. Can you fool people? Can you make people believe that you're really upset or crying or angry or laughing? It's a really fun game that a lot of people watch. Doing it well and honestly is challenging.

ON CONTINUING HIS ACTING CAREER

Ever since I started acting, I sort of convinced myself from the beginning it was just a hobby and people would say to me, "So you're going to be an actor." And I'd say, "No, no, no. Getting out of it. It's kind of this really cool hobby that I have." And I got older and more parts started coming to me and they were saying, "So you're going to be an actor — you're going to continue, right?" And I was still saying, "No, no, no, it would take all the fun out of it, I wouldn't want to do it." And it was only a couple months ago that I started thinking, "Who am I kidding? I do love doing it! If you can make a life out of doing your hobby, doing what you love, why not go for it?"

ON EXTRA-CURRICULAR ACTIVITIES

Four of my friends and I produce a radio show that plays throughout the school in the morning before class. We do political rock shows, mellow yellow, all kinds of music from reggae to hip-hop to heavy metal. We also have a debate show — one of my friends is a real lefty and another supports Bush, so they go head-to-head. It's pretty fun.

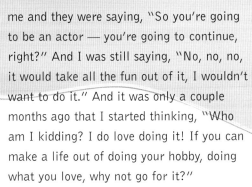

ON PLAYING THE BAD GUY

When I found out that I had to cheat on my girlfriend in the show, I was really upset. It was the first time ever that I've been a bad guy. I just wanted to talk the writers and say, "Why?"

ON WINNING A GEMINI AWARD

I didn't think I was going to win. I didn't prepare a speech. I totally made a fool out of myself. I was like "OH my GOD! I WON!"...I have a whole bunch of house league soccer trophies in my room, so I keep it next to them.

ON MUSIC

I love music. One of the guys from my old band and I played at a *Degrassi* wrap party, and I think that's why they started giving Craig more of a musical role. I played guitar in my old band, but now I'm the drummer for a band called Pin the Tail on the Funky. We've played a few gigs at school. For listening, I'm a classic rock guy. I like bands like The Beatles, Led Zeppelin, Jimi Hendrix, Pink Floyd, Simon and Garfunkel. What I like that's now are the Red Hot Chili Peppers, Coldplay....

ELLIE NASH

Played by Stacey Farber
born august 25, 1987

When we first met Ellie, she was in a dark place, dealing with her dad being overseas in the military and a mom who drank. She turned to cutting herself to control her pain. But help came to her from unexpected sources — first Sean, then Alex pointed her in the right direction. Of course there was always Marco, her best friend. And for a little while, there was even a ferret named Bueller....

ON JOINING THE SHOW IN ITS SECOND SEASON

It was difficult because everyone had already bonded and made their groups of friends. Fortunately, I knew Jake Epstein from school — he started a few episodes before I did — and he sort of helped me to get into it. The cast and crew on *Degrassi* have become a family. When you come onto set here, everyone is so friendly, whether they're in writing or production, cast or crew. Everyone knows everyone and it's a great feeling.

ON PLAYING ELLIE

A perk of being on a series for three or four years is that you really get a chance to grow with your character, unlike when you have a guest spot on a series, playing "girl number two" or whatever. I've been playing Ellie for three years now and the writers keep coming up with such great things for me to do as an actor. The fact that she's different from me makes it really exciting. Physically, we're different because she's the goth-ish character, and I don't dress like that in real life. There was also the whole story line where she was depressed and cutting, and though I know a lot of kids today do go through that, I don't and I didn't.

ON ELLIE'S LOOK

In the first couple of seasons, Ellie's look was more intense, and so hair and makeup took about an hour. There were streaks and black hairspray, lots of black eye makeup, different colored eyebrows and lots of piercings, but it's sort of been toned down over the years. Now it doesn't take as long. There's still the black eye makeup, but my hair is its natural color now. Ellie has matured a lot and, in real life, dressing the way Ellie does is usually a phase that only lasts a couple of years, so it seems more realistic.

ON BALANCING SCHOOL AND WORK

In my family, education has always been a priority. Right when I got into acting my parents said that I had to maintain good grades, so I've always worked really hard in school. Plus, I don't know how I could ever play the role of a high school student without ever attending a normal high school and having the experience of working with teachers and kids on that level.

ON MEETING THE FANS

My first big publicity event was in Texas with Miriam [McDonald] and we had to do a question and answer period. I was really nervous! I remember walking onto a stage and facing this huge audience to answer questions and I kept telling myself, "Be cool, be calm. Pretend to know what you're doing and that you've done this a million times." I had to pretend to be really confident when in my head it was, "This is ridiculous! What am I doing here?"

ON THE FUTURE

If I could be guaranteed work, I'd love to be an actor, but it's so risky. The work is unpredictable and so it can be scary making a living in this industry. My plan is to go to university and audition at the same time. I like writing — I've always thought it would be cool to write for a magazine. I like all that girly stuff.

TOBIAS "TOBY" ISAACS
Played by Jake Goldsbie
born august 8, 1988

Toby's not an unusual kid. He bugs his older stepsister, Ashley, to the point of distraction; he's occasionally at war with his best friend, J.T.; he stresses about his nerdy image; and he falls in love — or crush — too hard sometimes. But he stood out from the crowd when he stuck by Rick, having faith in Rick's change of heart when no one else would.

ON HIS START — AND ALMOST FINISH

I talked a lot as a child and so people told my parents that they should look into getting an agent for me, and that's exactly what happened. I played Chip, the teacup, in *Beauty and the Beast* on stage in Toronto for a while, and I did some commercials and voice work. I was actually starting to think of quitting acting when I got the call for *Degrassi*, and I'm so glad I didn't quit! I've found that the *Degrassi* cast and crew and the production company are the best people to work with in the world.

ON TOBY

He's a nerd, like the token computer geek, but I think there is another side to him that really comes out in the fourth season with the school shooting. He's really kind of happy-go-lucky — kind of a fun kid who just happens to enjoy computers more than sports. Toby tries to fit in with bigger kids, older kids, but is never quite able to find his place. Whether he's with J.T. or Rick, or trying to hang out with Jimmy, there's a really interesting character development there.

ON FILMING THE SHOOTING SCENE

I really enjoyed playing Rick's friend because working with Ephraim was just spectacular. That scene in the hallway where he is shot was the easiest acting I've ever had to do because he scared me as we were filming. That whole two weeks was a lot of fun because it was totally new to all of us. We'd all had dramatic plots before, but we'd never dealt with death. I think that's a *Degrassi* moment that people will remember and I am really happy that I was able to be a part of it.

ON BEING THE COMIC RELIEF

As much as I enjoy the dramatic Toby stuff, I thoroughly enjoy the subplot comic relief that Toby's brought to the series because I think it's just a lot of fun. I think that comic relief is so important in a show like this that deals with heavy issues. It makes it easier to watch, it lightens up the mood — not like breaking in and interrupting it, but it makes it so that not all things in life are über-dramatic.

ON ATTENDING AN ALTERNATIVE SCHOOL

My school caters to students who have other things going on, whether they are elite athletes, professional performers, or whatever. If you don't have a class, you don't have to be there and the classes are smaller. It's very one-on-one with the teachers, so if you miss something, you can catch up. I've found it's very difficult to be a working kid in a regular school. Our conversations are different from the ones at my old school. And it's nice to be able to continue that style of conversation whenever. It's hard to describe. I don't want to say it's more mature, because it's not. It's just different. We all have things that we do outside of school and we know what it's like to have something else on our plate. I enjoy that a lot more. It's not like I'm "the actor," since there are so many others.

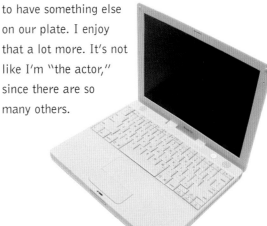

JAMES "JIMMY" BROOKS
Played by Aubrey Graham
born october 24, 1986

From basketball star being scouted by the big colleges to "the guy in the wheelchair," Jimmy has had quite a journey. But he has handled all obstacles with surprising confidence. His workaholic parents are seldom seen, but he has been able to find a great support group with his pals Marco, Craig, and Spinner — until the day Spinner went too far.

ON JIMMY

When I first met and became Jimmy, he was happy with his life, but was upset about his life at the same time, which was a position that I was in at that point in my life, so I think I brought a lot of myself to the character. Then, as the years progressed, the show gave me more confidence and I had the chance to hone my skills. I grew as a person, allowing my character to grow and expand. Now I see Jimmy as a more confident, level-headed guy with the right mind-set.

ON ACTING

This entire show has been a way for me to experience so many things, without facing the consequences. For me, that's what acting is. Acting is kind of a dream of mine that I'm finally achieving. When I saw *Devil in a Blue Dress*, I just fell in love with Denzel Washington, and I started watching all these other movies like *Mo' Better Blues* and all these Spike Lee movies. I wanted to know how it worked and how these people managed to do it all.

ON PREPARING FOR A ROLE IN A WHEELCHAIR

My neighbor works for a youth services program and knows this kid who used to play basketball and now he's in a

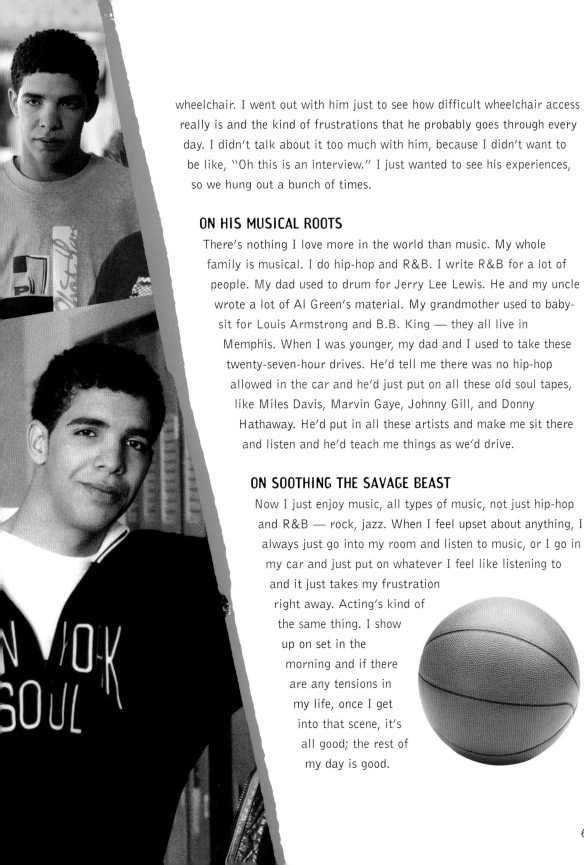

wheelchair. I went out with him just to see how difficult wheelchair access really is and the kind of frustrations that he probably goes through every day. I didn't talk about it too much with him, because I didn't want to be like, "Oh this is an interview." I just wanted to see his experiences, so we hung out a bunch of times.

ON HIS MUSICAL ROOTS

There's nothing I love more in the world than music. My whole family is musical. I do hip-hop and R&B. I write R&B for a lot of people. My dad used to drum for Jerry Lee Lewis. He and my uncle wrote a lot of Al Green's material. My grandmother used to baby-sit for Louis Armstrong and B.B. King — they all live in Memphis. When I was younger, my dad and I used to take these twenty-seven-hour drives. He'd tell me there was no hip-hop allowed in the car and he'd just put on all these old soul tapes, like Miles Davis, Marvin Gaye, Johnny Gill, and Donny Hathaway. He'd put in all these artists and make me sit there and listen and he'd teach me things as we'd drive.

ON SOOTHING THE SAVAGE BEAST

Now I just enjoy music, all types of music, not just hip-hop and R&B — rock, jazz. When I feel upset about anything, I always just go into my room and listen to music, or I go in my car and just put on whatever I feel like listening to and it just takes my frustration right away. Acting's kind of the same thing. I show up on set in the morning and if there are any tensions in my life, once I get into that scene, it's all good; the rest of my day is good.

GAVIN "SPINNER" MASON
Played by Shane Rippel
born june 4, 1986

Spinner started out at Degrassi as a one-dimensional bully, but he has since become that most complex of characters: the likeable bad boy. Sure, he wasn't always nice, but he was Paige's "Honeybee," so we could forgive him! When he helped execute the prank that led to the school shooting, and when he confessed his role and was expelled, we may not have been sure how to feel — but because it was Spinner, we cared.

ON BEING CAST

Degrassi was the third audition I had ever been to. I had my audition — two months later I had my callback, two days later I got the call from my agent telling me I got the job. It was kind of a thrill. I remember when I got the call for my first Degrassi audition that some of my friends were there and I said, "Hey, they're making a new Degrassi!" We were all pretty excited just about that, because we'd watched the old show.

ON SPINNER

He started out as a bully who was pretty much one-dimensional. He's kind of a tough guy. He's a little slow witted; you can see that when he thinks he has the right word, but it's the wrong word. He has a good heart, but he doesn't always do the right thing. He's really quick to react and really straightforward with what he thinks. He tends to get himself into lots of situations that he shouldn't have been in, just because he makes the wrong choices. He thinks of himself as a confident leader, but most of the time he's a follower. He's at that adolescent stage where he's almost found himself, but he hasn't quite yet.

ON BODY ART

The piercings Spinner has are my own. I asked the producers' permission before I did it. They've changed a little over the years. I have a couple of tattoos. [Points to his right arm.] This one's a phoenix. After I got it, my dad told me that a phoenix is a symbol for rising from the ashes when things fall apart, coming back stronger than before. Everyone has bad times in their life and I've been through a couple. It's kind of cool that after I got the tattoo, I can relate it to that, even though that's not the reason I got it in the first place.

ON BALANCING SCHOOL AND WORK

If you have difficulty figuring out what's important to you, then you will have problems doing it. If you want it badly enough, you can make it work. I think that's true for everything in life.

ON HIS FREE TIME

I do what any teenager would do. I party with my friends, I go to movies, I take acting lessons, I drum, I take drumming lessons, I'm at the gym five, six days a week. I'm in between bands because I'm trying to get to a point where I wouldn't feel I would be holding a band back. That's why I'm taking lessons. I'm trying to at least get to a point where I feel I could play any type of music. I'm working on singing. I sing in the car. People who drive next to me probably think I'm crazy. I sing along to CDs. It's fun to do that, because you try to not only hit the notes that these singers hit, but also change your vocal patterns to duplicate the style of singing, how raspy it is or how much of a whisper is incorporated. After *Degrassi*, you want to have as many things as you can on your résumé, make yourself as versatile as you can possibly be, so when someone looks at the résumé, it's just that more appealing.

HAZEL ADEN
Played by **Andrea Lewis**
born august 15, 1985

Hazel is on the Spirit Squad, cheering her heart out for the team — and that's just what she's like in the rest of her life. Hazel is always there for her friends, especially her boyfriend, Jimmy, and her best friend, Paige. Hazel once made the mistake of trying to hide her true self, but not anymore.

ON GETTING HER START

I started when I was a baby. My mom and I were in Yorkdale Mall in Toronto and some agent came over and said, "What a cute little kid!" and gave her a card. And then, after [Mom] thought about it for a while, she signed me up. I've done some commercials, movies — all that kind of stuff.

ON WHAT SHE LOVES ABOUT HER JOB

I mean, sure, the hours are long and sometimes we're given stuff we don't want to do — like when we're filming outside and it's supposed to be summer but it's actually November and we're freezing! I like that, that's just cool. When I think about other jobs that I could have as a teenager, I feel like I'm so lucky. Here it's like I'm not working. I'm with my friends all day and we're just having fun on set. There's nothing about it that I would want to change.

ON THE BEST PART

Probably the friends I've made working with the cast and crew; we're really close and we do a lot of hanging out outside of set. These are the friends that I'm going to have for the rest of my life. I'm very close friends with Adamo [Ruggiero], Lauren, Stacey, and Aubrey; those are my closest friends on the show. We go out a lot, talk on the phone, call each other.

ON FANS AND MALL TOURS

You never know how many people like the show. I'm the kind of person who, if you say a million viewers watched the show, I think, "Whatever." I don't really believe it until I

see it. But when you have a lot of people show up and they're excited, it makes you feel really cool. When somebody comes up to us with a Bristol board full of pictures — and not just pictures from *Degrassi*, but everything we've ever worked on — we realize that they like us, not just us as *Degrassi* characters, but us as actors, and that's a really nice feeling.

ON KEEPING IT REAL

When we were doing our *Teen People* shoot and we were going to New York, well, I was really excited, but when I called my friends to tell them, it was, "I'm not going to be here next week. I'm going to New York. There's this *Teen People* thing." I just make it very, you know, chill. Because of that, my friends have never really made a big deal of it. They find it funny or cute when someone recognizes me. My friend told me that one day she was at school and she was showing somebody one of her pictures in her wallet — we have a group picture of all of us together — and the girl yelled, "Oh my gosh! That's Hazel from *Degrassi*!" My friend laughed and said, "OK, calm down!"

ON HER RECORDING CAREER

By the end of 2004, I had two singles playing on the radio across Canada that I co-wrote with Justin Gray called "Superwoman" and "I'm Like (Ooh Oh)." I have also had a video for "Superwoman" playing on all of the MuchMusic stations, MTV Canada, and the Nickelodeon channels in the U.S. I've been singing just as long as I've been acting. They both have come very naturally to me. I started writing songs when I was about twelve and then I started taking it really seriously by working with different producers and trying to get my music out for everyone to hear!

ON HER MUSIC

My music is a mix of pop R&B/soul with an old school twist to it. I grew up listening to a lot of old soul music, legendary artists like Gladys Knight, and it really comes out in my own work. I had a show last summer and I invited Lauren and the gang. I sang old songs, like all these Motown hits. Afterward, Adamo said, "I should have told my parents. They really like this stuff."

With Hilary Duff
in Cadet Kelly

EMMA NELSON
Played by Miriam McDonald
born july 26, 1987

We first met Emma as a baby when she was born to Spike in *Degrassi Junior High*. Her mom married Mr. Simpson — one of Emma's own teachers! — and she has a new baby brother. An empassioned environmentalist, Emma is always throwing herself behind a cause or supporting an underdog. But as Emma hits the teenage years full force, a new kind of rebelliousness is boiling up inside her.

ON WHAT SHE LOVES ABOUT HER JOB

I love the experience, and the broad exposure — and on a show like *Degrassi* that's so issues-oriented, that doesn't skirt around things, we've got some leeway with what we're doing. We've got room to experiment a little bit more and to do things that are challenging, that require a lot of thought and depth and interpretation on different levels. Everything that we've done has been so incredible that ten years down the road, when I look at my career, the steps that *Degrassi* has taken me in will have played a phenomenally large part in getting me to where I eventually get with acting.

ON HOW HER LIFE HAS CHANGED

I think that the most challenging thing for me was the first season because I'd been hanging around for my whole life with the same group of kids, had the same routine. Everything was sort of one thing and then when *Degrassi* started, we moved to Toronto, I switched schools, I switched groups of friends, it was sort of a new starting point. So that was a sort of difficulty to...get a grounding, establish a new...idea of myself, or a new perception of who I am and where I want to take myself. It was...difficult making a transition. There are still things that are difficult about being an actor and being a student, but at the same time, it gives you a challenge and it gives you more perspective.

ON FRIENDSHIPS WITH THE CAST

I have very different relationships with all the different people. Cassie and I are good friends for sure, because we've been working together for four years and when she came into it, she was eleven and I was a little bit older and I kind of took her under my wing, and we've stayed close. I get along very well with all the members of the cast and they bring out different qualities in me and I think I bring out different qualities in them, and I think we're very lucky to have such a compatible cast.

ON BEING WOUNDED WHILE ON DUTY

Phil Earnshaw was directing, and he said, "OK, you've got to punch the door when you come in." There was a window in the door and I was supposed to be all emotional and so I punched, and instead of punching the frame, I punched the window! So I went to Emergency with this bloody wrist and of course, just my luck, I get recognized at the hospital by this little girl who wants an autograph.

ON GETTING RECOGNIZED

I get recognized pretty much daily. If I'm feeling grumpy, or I'm having an off day, I put on glasses and a hat and then I'm fine. But usually I like getting recognized because sometimes when you're shooting in a studio, it's very different from when you're on a stage and you get that immediate audience appreciation. You sort of forget what you're doing and then you do see the fans and you think, "Oh, my gosh, we're actually making a show and people actually watch it!" So I love getting recognized.

ON BEING ASKED FOR AN AUTOGRAPH WHEN THE FAN HAS NO PAPER OR PEN

That's happened once or twice, and I feel guilty if I don't have them either. We stop someone on the street and say, "Can we borrow a pen so we can sign something here?"

ASHLEY KERWIN
Played by Melissa McIntyre
born may 31, 1986

A poet and a musician, Ashley is very aware of the feelings of others — often more than they are about hers. A longstanding relationship with Jimmy ended, but her new relationship with Craig has been even more tumultuous and she's not sure how much more she can take. Her blended family is unusual. They all attended her dad's wedding to his male partner, where Ashley stood up for him.

ON BEING DISCOVERED

I've wanted to be an actor for as long as I can remember. My mom saw an ad for a community theater production and I continued acting as much as I could. The director of *The Secret Garden* had her agent come see our production and he wanted me to sign on. When he talked to me after the show, it's hard to describe the feeling. I just thought, "Oh my God! Finally, finally!" I knew this was my chance. I did a few small things and then I got the audition for *Degrassi*.

ON ASHLEY

She's really good at heart. She makes a lot of very stupid mistakes — a lot of it has to do with peer pressure — she's always feeling peer pressure. She's really smart. She's really talented and trying to find herself, trying to find her place in the world. We have a lot of similarities, but I'm more laid back, whereas Ashley stresses [laughs]. Well, I get stressed, too, but Ashley just deals with stress in different ways. She doesn't know how to relax. She shuts down — goes and hides in her room until it blows up in her face. I like to deal with things head on. Usually.

ON RETURNING TO SCHOOL

I want to start going to university because I don't want to be uneducated. I'm still trying to figure out what exactly I want to do. I definitely want to keep acting, but I also want to go to school. After I graduated from high school, I took a year off and I could feel my brain turning to blubber. I want to exercise my brain intellectually and I hope I can combine acting and going to school. Right now I'm leaning toward [studying] English, because that way I could get into writing and even scripts, which would be cool.

ON SINGING

I've been singing for as long as I can remember. Just recently, I've started getting into jazz. I'd kind of like to get into jazzy rock. I used to take piano lessons and since I stopped, I've found it hard to write songs as much as I used to. I used to sing at weddings, but lately my music has been mostly what you see on *Degrassi*. I've got to get a few more songs finished!

ON SUPPORT FROM HER FAMILY

My mom has been great, driving me in and out of town. We'd drive the two hours to a five-minute audition and then the two hours home again. She's been there every step of the way. During the shooting season, we'd come to Toronto and get a place short-term, and for six months she lived with me and drove me to work every day. She's been amazing. And my dad kept things going back at home and my brothers dealt with the fact that they didn't have a mom around as much. And they've all been really great.

ON SUPPORT FROM HER PETS

I've been living on my own, but now I have Morris, my toy poodle. He's the sweetest thing ever, and great company. And there's also my lop-eared rabbit, Harold.

MARCO DEL ROSSI
Played by Adamo Ruggiero
born june 9, 1986

Marco is best friends with Ellie, and he once wished he liked her as a girlfriend, but he just doesn't. Much of Marco's story revolves around him dealing with the fact that he is gay — coming out to family and friends; finding that some of those friends need time to deal; being true to himself in a relationship. It's a struggle that Marco is winning — for now.

ON JOINING THE SHOW IN THE SECOND SEASON

It's a great environment, but it was definitely a challenge for me at first. I felt like the new kid at school, except it was worse — not only did I have to find a way to fit in, I had to learn the business and the technical end of things, too. It was a big learning experience. What I've learned the most is all the jobs there are that I never knew about before.

ON HIS AUDITION

I initially auditioned for the part of Craig. Actually, the audition went pretty well, until they asked me to break-dance! I cannot break-dance!

ON WHY HE LOVES ACTING

I don't think any actors really know why they love it. I get to do things I can't do in real life. I'm a creative person and love to stretch my imagination. I get to learn about issues and about people. I love the glamour! I'm a guy for glamour. I love being in front of the camera.

ON MARCO

It's overwhelming, playing a teen struggling with his sexual orientation — it hadn't been done a lot before, and I was passionate about getting it right. He's a happy-go-lucky character on the surface, a peacekeeper among his friends. He seems to have all the ends tied: organizing dances, giving his friends advice. But Marco gets a little lost himself. He's so busy helping the others with their emotions that he doesn't deal with his own struggles. Spinner and Marco's relationship is one of the most powerful for me. The journey those two characters take together is very realistic.

ON THE RESPONSIBILITY OF PLAYING MARCO

With *Degrassi*, you get to hear the reactions after the show airs. It's hard when I get letters from kids revealing really intimate things about their lives — even suicidal thoughts. I'm not used to having an influence, and kids write and ask me for advice. I always write back because someone put a lot of trust in that letter. I tell them I don't have the answers for them, but there are people who do, people they can talk to.

acting, but it's not the only thing I'm interested in. I have other interests and strengths — I'm curious about journalism, advertising, anything kind of creative and media-related.

ON THE ISSUES

When we put the issues out there for the viewers, we are learning ourselves. We all want to work on something that's not going to be one-dimensional. We want to take it to a personal level so that kids out there realize they're not alone.

ON THE CHALLENGES OF ACTING

Sometimes you're put in a situation where you can try to understand, but you can't — you've never been there yourself. When that happens, I try to make it up in my mind and put it out there. It's important that the show is honest with the viewers.

ON SCHOOL

I'm studying English and Communications at university. Of course, my ideal is to keep

MANUELA "MANNY" SANTOS
Played by Cassie Steele

born december 2, 1989

The sweetest and most innocent of *Degrassi* characters at the start of the series, Manny has really grown up — and made serious mistakes along the way. First came her hottie makeover. Then she moved in on Ashley's boyfriend, Craig, but she paid a heavy price when she had to decide whether to have an abortion. Deep down, though, Manny just wants to be valued.

ON MANNY'S BOYFRIEND-THIEVING WAYS

I would be great friends with her in real life. Yeah, she does look like a boyfriend thief, but in the end, she's just Manny, and she's always treated her friends with respect. The boyfriend thief is understandable — just as long as it's not my boyfriend!

ON THE CHANGES OF HIGH SCHOOL

Everybody goes through different things when they get into high school. For instance, I was listening to a lot of R&B and hip-hop in elementary school, when everybody was listening to that one thing, and I never really knew about different kinds of music. And then when I got to high school, it was different. There were a whole bunch of different crowds and different things you could try, like a buffet, and I think that's why so many people go into a different level in high school. I still love R&B and hip-hop. But I like to sing alternative rock, jazzy, blues-y stuff. I like listening to metal, punk — there are so many things out there.

ON BEING TUTORED ON SET

I don't really like the tutoring. There are so many kids in the room. You don't want to work when you're already at work. You don't want to stress, because acting is mentally stressing. It's a lot of waiting around and then getting into character — it's really tiring, and when you're not needed on set, you want to go and lie down, read something, chill out, have a good time. Then they tell you that you have to go to the tutoring room. It's another energy drainer.

ON HER FUTURE

I definitely want to act and I want to sing. If those two fall through, I want to become a writer, probably, like a songwriter for other people, or a novel writer. I write a lot, and read a lot. I like reading fiction. Right now, my favorite author is probably Anne Rice. I'm just in the middle of her vampire books. I like mythology, anything historical.

ON HER ROOM

My bed is a double and I have a pink, fuzzy cover on it and black sheets. I have millions of pillows on my bed — millions! Velvety, I'm all about that. And then I have curtains around my bed, and they're black and lacy. And then I have this lip lamp and you can open and close the lips. And I have another lamp that looks like it has a spiderweb inside it. My walls are covered with posters of everything you could possibly think of, from cartoons to bands to ads and pictures. I have everything on my walls; it's like reading a magazine. And then I have this huge dresser. It looks like it should be in [Toronto castle] Casa Loma, it's so extravagant! It has a huge mirror and a million little drawers. It's amazing! I used to have a light blue carpet, but then I dyed it black, but it didn't quite turn out, so it's just dark blue now. That's what my room looks like. Nothing matches, but I love it.

TERRI McGREGGOR
Played by Christina Schmidt

born september 16, 1987

Terri has a terrible self-image. She's very pretty, but she thinks she's fat and that takes over everything. She let Paige use her. She settled for second-best and forgave her abusive boyfriend, Rick. When Terri finally recovered from her injury, she had to start over at a new school.

ON TERRI'S DEPARTURE

Some people think Terri's still in a coma, but she did recover — we saw her sitting up in hospital in "I Want Candy" in Season Three. But she would have had a lot of recovery still to come. And being the type of person she is, Terri would have switched schools. After all the drama of her coma and Rick's death, she would have found it really hard to go back to Degrassi, where people would have whispered about her.

ON THE ENTERTAINMENT INDUSTRY

Before *Degrassi*, I did some commercials and a movie. I had a leading role in a French TV series, working with Academy Award-winning director Brigitte Berman. I'm still going out on auditions and taking acting classes. I love the challenges of acting, but I'm also interested in behind-the-scenes positions, such as writing and producing. I hope to make my career in the entertainment industry.

ON BEING RECOGNIZED

My hair is dark now, so when people see me, they say, "You look just like that girl from *Degrassi!*" It's great because it's nice people recognize me, but on a day when I just feel more like hiding, I can.

ON BALANCING SCHOOL AND WORK

It would have been a challenge, but the tutors on set were great and all my teachers at my regular school were really supportive. I was able to fast-track and finished high school in three years. I even made the honor roll and had the highest English mark in grade twelve.

DYLAN MICHALCHUK
Played by John Bregar
born march 1, 1985

Paige's big brother is a charmer, an athlete, a generous, open soul — the perfect complement to shy, awkward Marco. As their relationship became more serious, Dylan was upset with Marco for not coming out to his parents, but ultimately, it was Dylan who let Marco down.

Mike Lobel

ON BEING PART OF TV'S PREMIER YOUNG GAY COUPLE

Oh, wow, yes, totally, I love that! Getting the role of Dylan, wow...I couldn't believe I was going to be part of such intense controversy — the first gay kiss on children's television!

ON PEOPLE ASKING HIM IF HE IS GAY OR STRAIGHT

I tell them that I'm a straight actor playing a gay role, and that I love playing the role. I don't want to leave people hanging. I'm not ashamed to say I'm straight! In the fourth season, I found myself being very comfortable kissing Adamo. For the first time, I didn't care what people thought. I was nervous and uncomfortable in the beginning, but as the scenes went on, it became more about making the moments real.

ON THE FUTURE

I've started writing, testing my creative side. I've had these scenes that pop up in my head while I'm driving and listening to Radiohead. I see the trees passing me and I have this moment of awareness and I just get this idea: I think, "Wow, this should be a scene." I'm writing down all these "freak" scenes and hopefully it will turn into something!

ALEX NUNEZ
Played by Deanna Casaluce
born february 7, 1986

We viewers are dying to know what makes Alex tick. She almost outed Marco, but she's also a pal to his best friend, Ellie. She helped to publicly humiliate Rick and she's mean to Emma — what's her story? We'll have to wait and see.

ON HER AUDITION

I auditioned and I got callbacks for both the characters Ashley and Paige. I thought for sure I had the best chance of being chosen, since I was up for two parts. But then I got neither! I was so discouraged, I stopped going out to auditions. I kept up doing theater at school and then one day — two years later — my agent called and told me I'd been cast in a new role. I was in shock! I was this chick, Alex, who steals and has a rebel boyfriend.

ON PLAYING ALEX

If I could ask to play one role and put all the personality characteristics and back story in, I would play Alex. She's everything I like in a role and if she were real, I'd probably be her best friend. A lot of the characters on *Degrassi* are somewhat close to the actors. I feel close to Alex — she's had her share of life experiences, she's smart and tough. I still have a lot more life experiences to go, but I understand her.

ON WHY SHE LOVES ACTING

Every person who has any passion gets a certain type of rewarding feeling when they're doing their passion. I don't know how to describe it — I feel accomplished. I have the feeling that I'm doing what I should be doing.

JAY HOGART

Played by Mike Lobel

born march 7, 1984

Jay is the truly dangerous bad boy of Degrassi. Long-time boyfriend of Alex, he cheated on her with more than one girl. He led Sean down the path of stealing, Spinner down the path of drinking, and Emma...even *he* wishes he hadn't corrupted Emma.

ON PLAYING THE BAD GUY

That character is a necessity. He causes problems that the main characters have to find something great and true in themselves to overcome. You have to definitely play him sympathetically because you can't have a bad guy for the sake of needing a bad guy. There must be some real motive under that. Humanizing him makes him even more threatening, scarier. The viewers know that there's something else there.

ON BEING RECOGNIZED

I'm always wearing that backward baseball cap in the show. I do wear caps in real life, but not backward. I get a lot of, "Did I go to school with you?" Then I take my hat and I'll turn it backward, and they'll go, "Oh, my God! You're the guy on *Degrassi*! You're *bad*."

ON HIS NEWEST MUSICAL INTEREST

I was shooting a film in Edmonton [Alberta], and I was away from all of my music; no guitar, no piano, no drums. When I went back to the hotel room, after about a week, I just was pulling my hair out. I decided to go out and find something, anything, I could play and write music with and which I could carry between Toronto and Edmonton. So I got a ukulele and a book and learned how to play it and I think it's a great instrument.

ON BEING PART OF THE SHOW

I don't think I will ever have an experience again where I'll be part of a show quite like this — with die-hard, long-time fans, even fans of the original who are now fans of the new generation. It's a huge deal, a huge part of Canadian culture, and I'm so grateful to be part of it.

DANNY VAN ZANDT
Played by **Dalmar Abuzeid** born october 23, 1990

Danny found it really hard to care about his snotty big sister, Liberty — especially when she was spending so much time with his dorky friend J.T. But Danny softened a bit when his dad came down on the new lovebirds like a ton of bricks.

ON AN ACTING CAREER

Sometimes it's intimidating working with the other actors because they have so much more experience. I worry about making a mistake. I know that if I want to be an actor for my career, I'll need a lot more training, and I want to get a proper education, too.

AMY
Played by **Bailey Corneal** born march 18, 1986

Amy's got a hard edge — she bullies Emma and she's willing to cheat with her best friend's boyfriend. What will we see from her in the future?

ON HER START

I started as a background performer in the first two seasons and then had a speaking part near the end of Season Three. The other background kids have been really supportive. It just goes to show that you can make it if you want something badly enough.

DARCY EDWARDS
Played by Shenae Grimes born october 25, 1990

Pretty, new girl Darcy actually kissed Rick — for a price. She had a lead role in the school play, too at least until she and J.T. had an argument over her diva-like ways.

ON JOINING THE CAST OF AN ESTABLISHED SHOW
It was so exciting, really cool, because I was already watching the show. My friends had also been watching it, so now seeing me on it is very weird for them. It was strange for me at first, too. I love being on set — the cast made it easy for me to fit in.

PETER STONE
Played by Jamie Johnston born july 7, 1989

Surprise! Principal Hatzilakos has a son! To the adults, new boy Peter is an angel: so charming and well-mannered, having been previously schooled in Europe. But when it's just the kids, Peter reveals that he's really a slick, smooth-talking devil who delights in being bad. Life at Degrassi will never be the same!

ON WHAT HE LIKED ABOUT TNG BEFORE HE JOINED
I enjoyed the story lines. You can never get bored with this show. I can really relate to some of the characters and I see reflections of my friends and classmates in many of them.

KENDRA MASON
Played by **Katie Lai** born september 1, 1989

Spinner's adopted, tomboy sister is a fistful of firecrackers. She had a relationship with Toby, but it didn't last very long.

ON HER START
I started in show business at the age of four, as one of the stand-ins in the stage musical *Miss Saigon* — as a boy!

ON TOMBOY KENDRA
In real life I'm quite feminine. But that's the fun of acting. You can expand your horizons. I find it fun to pretend to be someone I'm really not.

CHRIS SHARPE
Played by **Daniel Morrison** born october 29, 1986

Chris loves hip-hop and spinning tunes at the club where his cousin works. He has been a love interest/friend to both Emma and Liberty, but he turned on Emma when everyone heard what happened in the ravine.

ON BEING HIMSELF
I go to church, go to school, and play video games. I'd like to do more acting, but it's hard when you have to take a bus to an audition and miss a lot of school. I like having a little bit of fame, but I don't let it go to my head. It may not last forever, so it's important for me to do well in school.

ANGELA JEREMIAH
Played by Alex Steele born july 3, 1995

Joey Jeremiah's daughter, Angela, is a typical little girl who loves to play with her stuffed animals, skate, and spend time with her half-brother Craig. In real life, Alex is Cassie Steele's little sister. So when Craig says he has a problem with dating Manny because she reminds him of his sister — there's a good reason!

ON HER MENAGERIE
I like to play with my rabbit. His name's Cocoa. He's brown. He likes to hop around his cage and just lie down. I have two dogs and a fish. One of our dogs is Ozzie and one's Keanu. They're both big — one of them is bigger than me. The fish is called Tuffy because he pretty much ate every other fish in the tank.

HEATHER SINCLAIR birth date unknown

According to Paige, Heather's eyebrows are tragically overplucked and she has a major overbite. Heather was number two on Rick's list of desirable girls — right after Ms. Hatzilakos, so she can't be *too* bad looking! Her school dance theme ideas have included Hawaiian Surf Paradise and Celtic Winter Solstice. She is known as a serious cheese eater, as J.T. and Liberty decide to head to the cheese buffet "before Heather scarfs down all the Havarti." Heather made it onto the *Whack Your Brain* team, but she came down with mono and had to be replaced by her friend, Jimmy. She's a natural at yoga, says dreamy Mr. Oleander.

ON THE BAD BLOOD BETWEEN HER AND PAIGE
Heather was unavailable for comment.

MR. PERINO
Played by Tom Melissis

My *Degrassi* experience began with an appearance on *Degrassi Junior High* as an auto mechanic. I was born just a few blocks from Degrassi Street. Some ten years later, I was brought aboard Epitome's soap opera, *Riverdale*, and in one scene, I played opposite the Pat Mastroianni! I was slightly star-struck, but he was so down to earth, humorous, easy going, and a pro. The young actors I have worked with are also talented pros who are fun to hang with and very grounded.

MS. DAPHNE HATZILAKOS
Played by Melissa DiMarco

The producers make sure they reflect real stories of what teenagers go through. They explore the relationships that exist among students and teachers. The science material I was "teaching" in the Degrassi classroom was very similar to what the actors/students were studying in real life. It's great to see the special care taken to make the show that realistic.

MS. SAUVÉ
Played by Jennifer Podemski

I don't know any Canadian in my generation who didn't grow up watching *Degrassi*. It helped me feel like the things I was experiencing in my life were normal. I went to a performing arts high school that some of the *Degrassi* actors also attended. Although I was too star-struck to really have a normal conversation with any of them, they still inspired me from afar to go into acting. Little did I know that fifteen years later, many of these actors would become my peers.

MS. KWAN
Played by Linlyn Lue

Ms. Kwan is the mean teacher out of the lot. She was even referred to in one script as being "The Wrath of Kwan!" I hope I have been more effective as a friend on set to the cast and crew than Ms. Kwan is at Degrassi. I have been documenting the days I spent on *Degrassi* over the past four years. Most of the shots are goofy and have the cast members with their guard down.

The Teachers

MRS. NASH
Played by Kirsten Kiefferle

I was intimidated by the family/school-like feeling on set. But within hours I was so impressed by the respectful atmosphere. The crew are wonderful. They treat the young people with respect for who they are, but they don't forget that they're still children and need to be properly cared for.

MR. KERWIN
Played by Andrew Gillies

I had worked with Melissa before, so I was happy to find out I would be playing her father on *Degrassi*. There are few similarities between me and the character I play. The acting challenge was to show the courage of this man to be honest with his daughter. I was so impressed with the script writing that deals with a sensitive subject with great dignity. To work with [Director] Bruce McDonald again was a joy.

MRS. DEL ROSSI
Played by Brona Brown

I've had a great time being Marco's mom, and playing a character so different from myself in both comedic and dramatic scenes. What a really great experience! It's a well-run ship, and I can see why the show is so popular internationally. Stefan Scaini had directed me when I was seventeen; it was wonderful to work with him again.

MRS. KERWIN-ISAACS
Played by Maria Ricossa

Working with the kids on *Degrassi* has been a pure joy. I've loved being mother to Ashley and Toby. They are such a fine group of young actors and it's been a treat to see them grow and develop as people and professionals. It's a tribute to Linda and Stephen [Stohn] to have nurtured so many young actors' careers.

MR. DEL ROSSI
Played by Tony Sciara

Working with young actors is always fun and at the same time educational. As an actor, you base the development of your character, the emotions that will be brought out in your scene, on experiences that you've encountered. Watching these talented young actors develop their craft in front of the camera, working opposite them, is a learning experience. Even though they're young, they take the job very seriously.

Mr. Del Rossi is an old school type of guy with old school values, who wants to be proud of his only child. Imagine what's going to happen when he finds out that Marco is gay!

Guest Stars

DEGRASSI CLASSIC

In the late seventies and early eighties in Ontario, if you weren't out on a Saturday night, you were probably curled up in front of the TV for Elwy Yost's show, *Saturday Night at the Movies*. The man for whom the word "avuncular" might have been coined was the perfect slightly flustered judge in "Ida Makes a Movie" on *The Kids of Degrassi Street*.

Alannah Myles played Cookie's mom on *KDS* long before her singing career took off with the hit "Black Velvet."

Sue Johanson's *Sex with Sue* was a local radio show that inspired "Dr. Sally" in the episodes "Great Expectations" and "The Whole Truth" on *Degrassi Junior High*. Years later, on *Degrassi: The Next Generation*, she gave a sex education class to the students.

DEGRASSI: THE NEXT GENERATION

On *TNG*, higher profile performers occasionally appear. Well-known Canadian actor Don McKellar (at left) played some Hollywood guy named Keith who was dating Caitlin in the series launch special "Mother and Child Reunion."

Degrassi alumnus Bill Parrott decided not to return as Shane in "Father Figure," but we still needed Emma's dad! Who better than look-alike Jonathan Torrens, who had brought the cast together for a reunion on his show *Jonovision*?

With a few minutes' breather from his TV show *Doc*, country singer Billy Ray Cyrus turned in a few "achy breaky" laughs as Duke, the limo driver from your worst nightmare, in "The Power of Love."

When it was time for Sean to be goin' down the road home to Wasaga Beach, Jayne Eastwood was the mom to greet him. Jayne is an icon of Canadian film and television, having appeared in everything from the Canadian classic film *Goin' Down the Road* to the TV series *Road to Avonlea*.

Kevin Smith appeared as himself with his actor buddy Jason Mewes (at left) in a three-episode arc involving Caitlin. Singer Alanis Morissette (at center) plays the school principal in their fictional movie *Jay and Silent Bob Go Canadian, Eh?*, shot at Degrassi. Isn't it ironic she's Canadian? (If you've seen Kevin's films, you'll know what we mean.) Oh, snap!

You might think it's nothing but fancy guest stars up there on your TV screen, but when you're watching *Degrassi*, think again. Many of the adults the kids encounter in their day-to-day lives are people they already see every day — the crew! Here are just a few places you can spot them.

DEGRASSI CLASSIC

Producer Linda Schuyler steps in as a nurse in "Cookie Goes to Hospital" on *KDS*. You can frequently spot Linda as an unidentified teacher on *Degrassi Classic*, and that hard-hearted voice of Lucy's mom is hers, too. The patient in the wheelchair is Jimmy from Linda and Kit Hood's film, *Jimmy: Playing with Time*.

Yan Moore, writer and here, actor, found his motivation in the motto "I may be a louse, but I'll sell you a house" in "The Canards Move Out" from *KDS*.

That's this author as a book publicist in *DJH*: "What a Night!" What a stretch!

Art Director Judy Shiner seems to have found a way to save time and money on hair as a customer in Spike's mom's salon in *DJH*: "It's Late."

Rob de Lint is picture editor by day, a brutal condom cashier by another day in *DJH*: "Great Expectations."

Susin Nielsen, then craft services, was seen in the background as a caretaker in an early episode of *DJH*. When she became a writer for the series, she wound up with speaking parts as Louella in two different episodes — "Dog Days" and "Seasons Greetings."

Selene Strilesky, normally the script supervisor, shows us her previously unknown racy side, as a streetwalker in DH: "Little White Lies."

DEGRASSI: THE NEXT GENERATION

Watch out for the police! Line Producer David Lowe (with police cap) is often seen in uniform, and Derek Graham (at center), the props master, joins him in "Going Down the Road."

That big goof with the chewing gum as Kevin Smith's first assistant director in "Going Down the Road" is really Executive Producer Aaron Martin (at right).

There's Aaron again, with James Hurst (at left), story editor, in "Drive." Dolly Shanthakumar, assistant to the executive producers, was in that episode, too, as Joey's date.

Director Bruce McDonald pulls a Hitchcock, appearing somewhere in each episode he directs. In "Mother and Child Reunion," he arrives at the dance with Linda as his date. Here we see him directing another scene from this episode with Linda beside him.

Nearly everyone in the crew (who wanted to) appears somewhere in the various series. Watch for customers and clerks in stores, unidentified parents and teachers, police constables, passers-by, restaurant patrons, hospital patients, audience members — chances are if they're not crew, they're part of the *Degrassi* family!

3

Chapter 4

THE LOOK & SOUND

The *Degrassi* world may be a fictional one, but the people involved in creating this world — *Classic* and *TNG* — have gone to great lengths to make it look and sound realistic. You've met the creators, writers, and actors, now learn more about the magic of television through the eyes of the directors, cinematographers, set designers, wardrobe specialists, makeup artists, musicians, and sound engineers.

MAKING DEGRASSI: TNG

Putting together a single episode of TNG takes the hard work and dedication of the pre-production, production, and post-production teams, along with the more visible craft of the talented actors. Dozens of people work together to make the show you love. Fortunately, the people involved love what they do. It all starts with the story…

DEGRASSI: TNG DIRECTORS

Jim Allodi • John Bell • Anthony Browne • Graeme Campbell • Chris Deacon • Philip Earnshaw • Alan Eastman • Paul Fox • Anais Granofsky • Eleanore Lindo • Laurie Lynd • Bruce McDonald • Ron Murphy • Andrew Potter • Stefan Scaini • Gavin Smith • David Sutherland

PRE-PRODUCTION

Between seasons, the writers and producers map out season-long story arcs for the characters. For example, in Season Four, Craig is diagnosed with bipolar disorder and by the end of the season goes off his medication. The writers then collaboratively plan out where the story arc will be at any given point during the season.

Once the focus of an episode is decided, members of the story department work out the "beats" — the main events of the plot and subplot. It takes a long time to figure out what works and what doesn't. When Executive Producer Linda Schuyler has approved the story, it's written out into a "beat sheet" and approved by Linda and Executive Producer

(Creative) Aaron Martin (at left). The beat sheet is then converted into an outline, in which the story is laid out scene by scene. The outline, which includes the A plot and the B plot, is sent to the broadcasters (in this case, CTV and The N) for their input. Once the outline is approved by the broadcasters, a writer is assigned to write that script in full.

After a few drafts, a read-through of the script takes place with the cast. "Many directors are surprised when they hear what an extensive talk we have," says Aaron, "but it makes sense on this show to get the cast's input beyond dialogue, because we're adults trying to do kids' stories, and we want them to be able to say when things don't work. They know what it's like being a teenager now."

At this point, the director will take over from the story department, although any script changes throughout the process must be approved by the story editor. A concept meeting now takes place, in which the director sits down with the department heads and lets

PHILIP EARNSHAW
Director

Phil Earnshaw was the camera operator for *The Kids of Degrassi Street*, *Degrassi High*, *Degrassi Talks*, and *School's Out!* — and even directed some episodes. He came on to *Degrassi: The Next Generation* as a director. Although there have been many excellent directors on the show, Phil is the one most closely associated with it.

ON THE DIRECTOR'S TASK

The script is the skeleton and it's the director's job to put the muscle and flesh on that structure and to make it live. A director is an audience for the actors. You always have to keep your eyes peeled for things that don't seem real and strive to keep it real.

ON HIS ARTISTIC PROCESS

I'm a little uncomfortable with the "artist" word. It's kind of a crossover between craft and art because it's so technical. I think there's a certain art to helping an actor to give his or her best performance, and there's probably a certain art to getting the best out of a crew. Sometimes it's art, sometimes it's politics.

them know whether special sets will be needed (for example, decorations for a dance in the gym), so that they can begin to prep. Most episodes are prepped for four days — double episodes for eight.

Now, the director begins the serious planning of how to shoot the scene. "Let's say there's a scene in the cafeteria," explains Director Phil Earnshaw. "I'll go over to the cafeteria and figure out who is talking, where they are going to sit, and how the camera is going to pan around. The actual words on the page are the starting point for how I'm going to block a whole scene. The nice thing about *Degrassi*, as opposed to other shows, is that the script is usually pretty close to its final shape when you start prep. I keep a little book and I have little maps. I write down where the camera is going to be and how many shots [there will be] in each direction, and I figure out what lighting has to happen. By the end of the prep period, I know that I have 80 [camera] setups and 120 shots, or however it works out."

Meanwhile, the first assistant director (1st AD) makes a schedule indicating which scenes will be shot on which days. The director will go over it, seeing how many shots the crew will have to do each day and make suggestions if the schedule seems too uneven. "The 1st AD is the director's right hand — the person who takes on all the logistical challenges of the schedule, the liaising between departments, the running of the floor when shooting," explains Phil. "We started out with Stephanie Cohen; later Mark Pancer along with Derby Crewe, who has been with us throughout. They are very important people," Phil says appreciatively. "Their job is very different from that of the director in that theirs is mostly an organizational job and the director's is mostly a creative job. Avra Fein, our 2nd AD, is usually the one doing the paperwork, and our 3rd AD, P.J. Diaz, is usually the one on set keeping track of the background performers. We had

Siluck Saysanasy, who played Yick on *Degrassi Classic*, for our 3rd AD for the first three years."

Next comes a production meeting where all the department heads go through the script one scene at a time, making sure everything is in place and everybody knows what to do. The director will then have a "tone meeting" with the producer and writer. "It's the best meeting of all," Phil enthuses. "You talk about the feeling of the scenes and the emotional tone. It's your last chance to really nail what the producer's and writer's intent is, so that you make the producer happy and you get hired again!"

The cast of *TNG* has a round of rehearsals on the second last day of prep. Most other shows do not do this. "It was something that Kit and Linda understood very early on as being extremely helpful," explains Phil. "It's a huge advantage to get that rehearsal time, because it cuts down on the amount of time on the days of shooting and gives you a chance to get to the heart of the scene without all the pressures of production breathing down your neck."

While Phil is getting ready for the shoot, Production Designer Stephen Stanley is hard at work creating the look for the episode. "The production designer's job is to create a film environment that works for the show and the technicians, looks good, and is on time and on budget," says Stephen. "I first see a script at the outline stage and I get all outlines and drafts as the writers prepare them. With a short prep time, this lets me know what is coming down the pipe to get me thinking 'big picture' about what will need to be done. I also can make suggestions or raise flags about possible problems early in the creative process."

A pre-concept meeting is held between Linda, the writers, the production manager, and the production designer to talk "broad strokes" on what the episode will look like. When the script is fleshed out, the art department makes a

Anais directs.

Director
Graeme Campbell

detailed breakdown, listing all requirements scene by scene and department by department. "Now things have to move quickly, with only eight days before we start to shoot," Stephen explains. "And remember, we are shooting two episodes while we prep the next two episodes!" Stephen comes up with concept sketches for all sets and design requirements. He meets with his assistant art directors, Melinda Sutton and Sean McLoughlin, who get started on detailed build drawings for Murray Lowe, the construction coordinator. They then choose all paint finishes for Cameron Hoffman, the key scenic artist, and discuss and plan the decorating of the sets with Set Decorator Gabriel Lamb.

Stephen checks in regularly with David Lowe, the line producer and production manager, and with Gavin Smith, the director of photography, for any lighting concerns. He also works with Max MacDonald, the assistant art director, who designs the bulk of the graphics for the show, such as signs, tickets, posters, and so on. Graphics for the computer screens you see in the Media Immersion Lab on the show are animated and operated on set by Matt O'Sullivan.

Props Master Derek Graham meets with Stephen to work through all the prop requirements for the episode. "It's supremely important that everything works and it's safe for our actors and crew, but still looks believable for the audience," says Derek. "For instance, on *Degrassi*, we don't usually deal with swords. We ended up with three sets of swords [for the Canadian ninjas in "Going Down the Road"] — real ones for research, wooden ones for the fighting (since the clanging sound goes in later), and plastic ones for looks and safety."

Stephen's job doesn't stop there, though. "I also coordinate with SPFX [special effects] and stunts to work out special gags like fires, explosions, and car accidents — discussing how these will look, work, and what is needed from all the departments to get this done while addressing all the safety issues. I also choose vehicles with the transport coordinator and director, and talk to Costume Designer Melanie Jennings and let her know our color palette so sets and wardrobe work together. At the same time, I am scouting with Location Manager Greg Holmgren, the director, and 1st AD, and dealing with all the construction, paint, and dressing issues that are necessary on location. And, of course, I have to stay flexible because the schedule and the script are always changing!"

PRODUCTION

At last, filming begins! A major factor in filming a scene is the ambient sound. "There are some noises that are OK to hear," says Sound Recordist Dan Latour, "but there are other noises that are just unacceptable. We had a scene where Craig is developing music in the boiler room in the school, which actually is the real boiler room for Epitome. Everyone in production fell in love with the set...but it was disastrous for sound because there are several transformers in there that power essential services around the building. Those transformers are very noisy and the room had this terrible buzz to it. We'd had experience with a computer system for removing noises from sound recordings and I suggested we hire this system. It made it sound like we'd just turned all these electrical transformers off. Ironically, in the finished show, sound editorial had to edit back in a faint buzzing

Director
Ron Murphy

GAVIN SMITH
Director of Photography

Gavin has worked in music videos, commercials, and TV movies. One of those movies included scenes in a high school. Linda Schuyler liked what she saw and Gavin was hired as the director of photography for TNG.

ON THE EFFECT HE TRIES TO CREATE

I like to base my cinematography on storytelling. It's not about being glamorous. The camera, and the way it moves, has to feel like one of the other kids. We want viewers to feel like they're another kid in the school.

ON WORKING WITH YOUNG ACTORS

Kids have a lot of energy. Assuming that right from the beginning, I tried to have the camera emulate that so when you do cut it together, it doesn't look like you're trying to control these kids too much. I think that some television has the danger of looking very stagy — that people just conveniently hit their mark and speak back and forth. There is still that in *Degrassi* — to service the script you need that — but I try to get away from it. To make it look like it "just happened" is more of a challenge than anything.

ON WHEN IT'S WORKING RIGHT

When it's done really well, you can't recognize it, you just feel it. The cinematography is as much about feeling something as looking at something. The really successful parts of cinematography, in my mind, are not even the kind that win awards.

noise to create a believable 'soundscape' for the scene — but it is nothing like the reality of the live set."

Camera Operator Mark Hroch, 1st Camera Assistant Kaelin McCowan, and 2nd Camera Assistant Dennis Kim set up and operate the cameras. You won't see too many fancy gimmicks in the camera work. "*Degrassi* stays a little bit truer to its roots, or truer to reality," explains Director of Photography Gavin Smith. "It doesn't use a lot of that extra camera language. It's using the simple tools...just everyday cameras, lenses, shooting at regular speed. Rarely would we use slow motion. The style of the show is not about anything weird you can do with the camera. It's about using the camera strictly to tell the story."

There are two teams that deal with lighting: the electrics and the grips. The electrics set up all the lights and power, and the grips shape it by setting up surfaces upon which to reflect and focus the light. These teams work hard to make the light look as natural as possible.

At the end of a shooting day, the director can watch the dailies — the tapes of the day's filming. But Phil usually chooses not to. "I've seen it all as we are filming, so I know what's there," he says. "I'll watch if I'm unsure of a performance, but it doesn't happen all that often, because I'm usually already aware of it as we go."

POST-PRODUCTION

Post-production is where the editor's job begins. He or she will put together a twenty-five-to-thirty-minute-long "assembly," which will be sent to the director a few days after the filming of an episode. "Generally, I'm the one choosing the performances with the rushes or dailies," says Editor Stephen Withrow. "I make notes of performances and technical camera issues and I assemble it using my instincts. Generally, they turn out not to be too far off what the director had in mind for the intent and flow of the scene." Perhaps not too far off, but the director still has some input to make. As Phil explains, "Sometimes I might have expected to use a different take, so I'll go back to the rushes and say, 'Try using take three on that one.'"

So Phil and Stephen sit down and do the director's cut. "Then my responsibility as a director is over," says Phil. Now it's up to Stephen to make the fine cut to get the show down to standard twenty-two minutes. "A half-hour episode is about a minute a page of script, and it's always written a little bit heavy [long]. It's a collaborative process — I get notes from the writers and from the broadcasters at the fine-cut stage," explains Stephen.

Once the show is picture locked, which means no more changes will be made, it's handed off to the sound, video,

Stephen Withrow

103

Ella ↗

↖ Dave

↙ Jake in ADR

and music people. Composer Jim McGrath watches the episode with Linda, Stephen Stohn, and Executive in Charge of Post Production Ella Schwarzman. They decide what music is needed, when it should start, when it should end, and what style it should be. Then, Jim writes and records the score. Music Supervisor Jody Colero decides how the score will fit in. Everyone listens to what Jim has written in a music playback session, fixes are made if necessary, and then it goes to the final mix.

Meanwhile, Assistant Editor Gillian Truster makes a "cutting copy" of the episode, which is used as a guide for both audio and video. On the video side, every shot is replaced exactly the way it is on the guide with the same material, using the high-definition (HD) master tapes, which are much better quality. This is called a video conform or online. The video conform is cleaned for dirt on the negative, color-corrected, and then packaged with all the fades, head and tail credits, generic opening, and any special effects that are needed for the episode — just the way you see it on TV.

On the audio side, other parts of the soundtrack are being finalized. Danielle McBride cuts together all the dialogue so it is clean and intelligible, while Dave Moffat creates the soundscape for the scene. If the sound recordist hasn't been able to capture the dialogue cleanly enough, Additional Dialogue Recording or Automatic Dialogue Replacement (ADR) will be ordered. For example, Jake Epstein did some ADR for episodes 421/422, or "Going Down the Road, Parts 1 and 2." To keep the same feeling as the original scene, Jake moved from side to side as he did in the original shot. But to avoid getting clothes-rustling sounds, he kept his arms away from his body. "It's sometimes hard to get the actors to get back into the frame of mind to recreate emotional or difficult scenes," Danielle confesses, "but I love it all. I love sculpting the audio and putting in all the little nuances — background conversations, sounds of hallways and crowds — things you wouldn't notice, but you'd miss them if they weren't there." Dave agrees: "In the scene where Caitlin and Kevin Smith are in the bar, it would have been very quiet on the set to get the dialogue, so I have laid in glass clinks, ice tinkle, background conversation sounds, a cash register, and beer pouring. You don't see any of this, but it all helps make you believe you are in a bar with the characters."

The rest of the sounds, such as footsteps, setting down a teacup, catching a ball, or fighting ninjas with swords are created by the foley artist, Virginia Storey. She has a suitcase filled with props, a huge pile of different shoes, and a variety of floor surfaces for creating footsteps in different environments. Virginia gets help from Foley Assistant Jennifer Brath. Sometimes Jenny joins Virginia in the studio to create more complicated sounds, while Foley Engineer Eric Culp records it all.

The sound mix is where it all comes together; where the beautiful, clean dialogue is placed into its environment of sound effects, foley, and music. Mike Baskerville keeps his ear on dialogue and music, which are the most important "stems" in drama, as they carry the emotion and the story. Paul Williamson checks on sound effects and foley, which are the stems that make the environment seem real and help you believe in the story. Together, they mix the sound till the blend is just right.

At last, the show is ready to be "restriped" — when the mix and fixes are complete and sound stripes are put on the master HD tapes. The dialogue is on a separate track from other sounds, so that when the show is dubbed into other languages, the other sounds are not affected. The finishing touches are done and the episode is finally ready for the broadcaster — and your viewing pleasure!

Virginia

Eric

Mike, Paul

MAKE A DEGRASSI PILGRIMAGE

If you are visiting Toronto, you can see the locations where *Degrassi Classic* was filmed. Sorry, TNGers, your show is shot on a special lot (see page 112). For you time trippers, get yourself a day pass on the TTC (local transit) and you can ride all over Toronto for the day on the buses, subways, and the iconic streetcars — pretend you're Kathleen, Melanie, and Diana going to the movies!

Start by visiting Degrassi Junior High. You can get there by taking the subway to the Kipling station and taking the Kipling bus south to Birmingham Street (ask the driver — it's just north of Lakeshore Boulevard). Walk west on Birmingham to 24th, turn left, and go one block to Daisy Avenue. Turn right on Daisy Avenue and you will see the school up ahead on the right.

It's now Vincent Massey Public School but, at the time, it was Daisy Avenue Public School. The school was not being used by the local board — there was a private school on the ground floor and

Degrassi was shot mostly on the second floor and outside, although the ground floor gym was used for dances and the front entrance was occasionally pressed into service when the private school was not in session. On the second floor is a single hallway with four main rooms: two were used as classrooms, one doubled as the green room and the "library," and the fourth was partitioned into two dressing rooms and a makeup and costume area. A smaller room was used as the office — Mr. Lawrence's door opened onto a blank wall! — and another room opposite this was used for preparing snacks and lunches. By moving the lockers into different configurations, the crew created the illusion of various hallways.

When you've finished looking around outside, walk south a block to Lakeshore Boulevard. Cross the street and climb aboard an eastbound 501 streetcar. The ride takes a while, but it travels through some of the most interesting parts of Toronto, so enjoy, and make note of places you want to see more of another day. Keep your eyes peeled after you pass Bathurst Street. On the left, at the corner of Augusta Street is the Duke of Connaught, where Wheels' dad had a gig in "Parents Night." (If you want to see where he played in "Taking Off," you have to go to Port Hope, Ontario. Yes, it's a real place!) After Yonge Street, keep an eye on your left for St. Michael's Hospital, where all the Degrassi Classic hospital scenes were shot.

Once you cross the Don River Valley, you're in solid Degrassi territory. Hop off the streetcar any time after Broadview Avenue to explore the area on foot. Spike's mom's hair salon was along this stretch, and so was the clinic where Spike found out she was pregnant, and the twins went when they thought they had mono. That clinic, on the corner of

Strange Street, has been replaced by a small office building. Look to your left, and there's Degrassi Street, running north from Queen Street.

Take a stroll along Degrassi Street, where you can visit Bruce Mackey Park and read the plaques. This was the park where Michelle, B.L.T., Alexa, and Simon had lunch in "Loyalties." If you watched *The Kids of Degrassi Street*, you may recognize the houses where Ida, Noel, and Cookie lived, but if you're of a later vintage, you won't spot many landmarks here. The Degrassi Grocery, which was a real corner store, has been converted into a private home. Glance to your left at Cummings Street and you will see the school that stood in for Degrassi Junior High in background shots. That's really Dundas Street Public School, where *KDS* shot school scenes.

Head back down to Queen Street and continue walking east. On your left, at 932, is a restaurant that used to be called 13 Busy St., where Melanie showed off her newly unbraced teeth, Joey had Coke dumped on him by Caitlin, and where he took Tessa after the movie. Across the street is L.D.'s dad's garage — Tom Melissis, who now plays Mr. Perino on *TNG*, played Jeff, the mechanic, here.

Just ahead is the corner of Queen and Carlaw, prime *Degrassi* land. On the left is the Shopper's Drug Mart, the store that sold all the condoms and pregnancy kits, and

employed Joey in the fateful summer of *School's Out!* Keep your eyes open in this area for the office that stood in as the abortion clinic the twins visited. Directly opposite, and next to the gas station, is the former office of Playing With Time, where every episode was planned and the actors met every day to be taken to whatever set they were filming on in a minibus. Behind that building was where Ida, Cookie, and Noel's clubhouse stood, now long gone.

On the northeast corner is the Celline Garden Restaurant, where Pat went for dinner on his "Day in the Life" (see page 19) and Pete waited for his date in "Griff Makes a Date." Up the fire escape is the original office of Playing With Time, which was also Kit and Linda's home in the early days. In TV land, it was also where Griff (KDS) and Rick (DJH) lived.

Just a block north is the short Colgate Avenue and a vestige of the factory seen in "Smokescreen," but right now, you want to walk a little farther east and you may see the house where the workshops for *Degrassi Classic* were held, and some location filming took place.

Go north now, and you might see a few location homes. Please remember, these are all private homes, some once owned by the production, but none are connected in any way with *Degrassi* now. So do the polite thing and don't bother the residents! Interiors and exteriors of these buildings were used as homes — but the twins' bedroom was in the same house as

Joey's kitchen, and Caitlin's bedroom was several miles from her living room! The house that was Lucy's exterior and party central inside was actually Kit and Linda's home at the time.

At Gerrard and Pape, you can see Gerrard Square, where Joey and Tessa made out in a car in the parking lot, and whose interior is the inspiration for the mall set on *TNG*. The pedestrian overpass is where Lisa tried to roller skate in "Pete Takes a Chance." Walk west for two blocks to Carlaw to see the Rose Donut Shop where Michelle worked.

If you are tired of walking, whip out your day pass and jump on the bus to the Pape subway station. If you decide to walk, go straight north on Carlaw and you will come to Withrow Park, the park seen most on *KDS*, and the site of Joey's beating in "Fight!" It was also an interview location for *Degrassi Talks*.

If you want, you can even wander east from the park to Earl Grey Senior Public School on Strathcona, where Bruce and Linda taught and many of the young actors attended classes. It also played the high school Clutch and Paul attended and its cafeteria was in "Season's Greetings." The playground where Lucy and Clutch talked is across the street.

Kit and Linda and many of the actors and crew lived in this area when *Degrassi Classic* was in production.

If you are on foot, you need to go two blocks east when you get to Danforth and turn north on Pape Avenue to get to the subway station. Or, if you still feel like walking, you can continue north on Carlaw. A northbound Pape bus will take you to Mortimer Avenue. Go a block west and there it is — Degrassi High! The building used to be a teachers' college, and incidentally, was where the auditions were held for "Ida Makes a Movie."

The building is now part of Centennial College, a post-secondary institution. You can go inside and see the courtyard, the ramp, the three-windowed doors, and the familiar brickwork and glass that inspired the set of TNG.

You know how to get back to the subway — it's south. Is it dinner time? The Danforth area has a great restaurant row!

HOW DEGRASSI STREET GOT ITS NAME

Captain Filippo De Grassi was an Italian soldier who fought for both the British and the French in the early nineteenth century, but ended up on the British side. With the promise of land in Upper Canada, he emigrated and settled in Toronto in 1831. He became a member of the infamous Family Compact, an elite group that ran the government.

A HECK

Take a tour of the *Degrassi: The Next Generation* set with Designer
Tamara Deverell and Production Designer Stephen Stanley.

Unlike the previous *Degrassi* series, *Degrassi: The Next Generation* is mostly
filmed at the Epitome Pictures studio that was originally created for
the soap opera *Riverdale*. Tamara Deverell, a top artistic director for film
and television, was hired to convert the studio into a school.

STUDIO C

Some alterations have been made to the school set since Tamara
worked on it. A stairway and balcony were added to the foyer as the
show's growing budget made them possible.

OF A LOT

Stephen: The balcony and stairs are our attempt to get people up off the floor instead of having all the people's heads in the same plane. We can put the camera up there to open things up, create more space, with the camera shooting down.

My task on *Degrassi* is to make it look like what our world looks like. Everything has to be researched. What lines would appear on a gym floor? What do kitchen cabinets look like? You just can't invent what a record store looks like or what a hospital sign looks like. Everything has to be researched and then tailored to work with what our show looks like, what the colors of the show are, what the colors of the characters are, and what the feel is.

Gym

Tamara: Initially, we laid flooring down for the gym, but it warped, so we ended up painting the floor directly onto the concrete. We put the school colors and banners on the wall. And then, we developed markings on the floor for the various sports.

Media Arts Classroom

Tamara: The windows and doors of the media arts class were from the set of *Death to Smoochie*, a movie I was working on when Linda called me. They gimbal, or turn, on an axis. You can prevent the reflection of the camera crew that way, just with a small turn. I believe they pop right out if you need to shoot into the classroom from a bit more distance.

Lockers

Tamara: Normally, I'm not one of the people who goes out and buys things for sets, but the show's set decoration department wasn't in place yet and we had to get the lockers in order to build them into the walls. They were from a hospital — very colorful.

STUDIO B
Emma's Room

Stephen: When Emma moved to the basement because of the new baby, my brother had just bought a little house. I was standing in the basement at his place and I thought, "Perfect." So this space is modeled after my brother's house (see page 120). We've put Emma in an uncomfortable situation, and yet we've provided her with a place where she can have privacy. It's also darker, as her character is changing.

Ceilings and Walls

Stephen: Here's a ceiling flat made of canvas used for Joey's living room. This one sort of matches the exterior, but while the one on the back lot is 75%-sized, this one is maybe 125% — for crew access and comfort. All the walls are "wild" — every wall can be removed to set up lighting and other equipment. You have to warn the directors not to shoot the whole thing, otherwise the interior size won't match the exterior size and it won't feel right.

The perfect human being is all human

Floors

Stephen: People are always fascinated by the scenic treatments painted on our floors.

STUDIO A

School Walls

Tamara: We put up these sayings because we wanted to make this school look a little more creative. I saw that at the Etobicoke School for the Arts, which was one of the schools I visited for research.

Classroom Doors

Tamara: These doors with windows — a detail from Centennial College — turned out to be a problem because whether you're filming in the classroom or the hall, you need to show action both inside and outside the room, which just makes it more complicated.

English Classroom

Stephen: Right now this class looks neat and orderly, but when we are shooting, the classrooms are very messy for a deliberate contrast to other parts of the school.

Washrooms

Tamara: What a great washroom to shoot in — you couldn't build a set that has as much room to shoot in. We use this for both the girls' and boys' washrooms. They bring urinals in when it's the boys' room and remove them for the girls' room. It's painted beige so it is gender neutral. To make it look more like an authentic school washroom, we added graffiti.

Cafeteria

Stephen: The cafeteria is meant to be a really boring space. The school really does film well. It's a beautiful school and I thought we needed a space that was really bland and this is it. I thought it would take the edge off the school appearing too high end. Most schools, really, they look like prisons. We don't want Degrassi to feel like a prison, but we also don't want it to feel like a high-end designer school. When we're shooting in the cafeteria, Derek Graham, our props master, devises all these horrible concoctions to serve as food. This is also where the cast and crew really eat lunch!

BACK LOT
School Exterior

Tamara: This was the really hard part — can we make this into a high school? We went to Centennial College [where *Degrassi High* was filmed], and we actually used the same colors and glass pattern for the facade. We had to cut larger window holes into the existing building, even on the second floor, which isn't part of the set, but looks like it from the outside.

Of course, this is a real building, not a film set. Everything we did had to be real and engineered. Usually, the design is all fakery, but when you're dealing with a real building, of course, you're dealing with real structure. For example, we had to place the post in the middle of the school's front doorway. I normally wouldn't do something like that, but we had to conform to real building codes, so the place won't fall down over the years.

We had professional tradespeople come in to do the stairs and this entire sidewalk. We had to pour concrete, keeping enough room to get vehicles through. This meant we had to obtain the right permits and follow City Hall codes.

Up there, that's the original banner. I can't believe it has survived.

Then there are the Degrassi Community School letters. Normally, we'd order them from a company that does all the cut-out letters for movies and TV that are fake and are not made to last. For these, I had to go to a real sign company. The letters have stood the test of time.

Over here, where the classrooms are, I wanted to have solid windows right across. But the engineer came to us and said, "No you can't legally have the windows more than a certain

percentage of the brick area." So I made the windows within a quarter inch of the maximum size, because for filming, it's all about having an abundance of light.

Stephen: This is where they shot the first season of *The Next Generation* [points to front of the school]. And then I thought we should make this area an entire environment. So we put a hoarding area in front here facing the school. We continued with these glass panels, put the chain link up, and got a bus shelter. Now we're able to shoot the whole school environment. Out of the eighty-eight shooting days we have, we shoot six or seven days on location and the rest of the time here. I don't think *TNG* looks like a studio show because we also have this back lot.

House Exteriors
Stephen: All the house exteriors that we shoot are here on our back lot, but we never shoot so you can see both sides of the street.

This building plays both Spinner's house and Liberty's house. There's very little space here, but, by cheating camera angles, we just manage to build a world that I think feels much more spacious than it actually is.

The houses on the back lot are all about to three-quarter scale. We've built little rooms inside some of them. There's the garage where Craig's band rehearses. But the inside of the bigger garage is where we actually shoot.

People are always surprised about the front and the back of these buildings. For example, this is Sean's hovel.

SET DECORATION: CHARACTERS' BEDROOMS

A *Degrassi* character's bedroom is the most telling set for that character — their inner sanctum tells a lot about their inner workings. Most teens have one foot in childhood and the other in adulthood. Art directors create spaces that look right for each character and add visual details to make the character pop from the script's page.

JUDY SHINER Art Director, Degrassi Classic

ON CREATING BEDROOMS

They were a lot of work, because we had to wash and iron sheets so they would look natural. We had to cram so much stuff into what would turn out to be maybe a thirty-second scene.

ON LUCY'S ROOM

You can see the teddy bears Lucy hasn't quite left behind. Lucy's about style, so we can see her wardrobe, a hat collection, scarves — the scarf colors pick up from the dress she's wearing. The neutral tones in the walls were chosen to set off Anais's skin color. Her snow globe collection adds a touch of whimsy and fun that's very

Lucy. The bed isn't made, because it wouldn't show in the shot. Lucy's bedroom was actually just drywall set up in the school library. She's on the same bed you see many of the other

characters sitting on. The poster of the palm tree might have been hand-drawn — we always had to be careful not to use things in the background that had copyrights attached to them.

ON LIZ'S DREAM SEQUENCE ROOM

In "Crossed Wires," Liz has nightmares about her childhood, when she was sexually abused by her mother's boyfriend. We did everything to make the young Liz seem as small as possible. This was also a bedroom created in the school with drywall, so we made all dimensions larger than life. The door through which the man enters is huge! We included lots of kiddie things, like the rocking chair and the romantic poster. Everything came from second-hand stores, except that same bed. We used blue for a cool, almost cold atmosphere. For the older Liz's bedroom, we kept the elements similar, but changed the proportions, colors, and the bed headboard.

ON ARTHUR'S ROOM

Here for "Dream On," we brought back stuff we'd used in earlier episodes. There are all his practical joke items from "Making Whoopee," like the snake in the peanut can, the oversize glasses, and a teddy bear — but also a Gourmet Scum poster, a bulletin board, an anti-acne cleanser...things to show he's developing more grown-up habits and tastes. He's sleeping on a dark sheet, which is unusual, because it absorbs light and doesn't necessarily flatter the skin tones.

STEPHEN STANLEY
Production Designer, TNG

ON MOVING EMMA'S BEDROOM

When her brother, Jack, was born, Emma's room on the second floor became the nursery. In a small, two bedroom house, where would she go? We decided to put her in a raw, unfinished basement — to put Emma in a dramatically uncomfortable setting that would make viewers feel sympathy for her and reflect the chaos that was her family life with a new baby in the house. It is an intentionally awkward, ugly, realistic-looking, utilitarian set.

ON THE ELEMENTS OF THIS SPECIAL SET

❶ The wall colors are a liver pink and a lime green, as if they were painted with what was left over from previous paint jobs. ❷ To enhance the realism, we filled the ceiling with cable, wiring, and pipes (one of which drips on Emma while she is in bed). We must have done a convincing job because when the electrical inspector was checking our studio, he was surprised when the set dressers told him it was all fake and that none of it worked. ❸ The only natural light comes from small high windows where there are window wells. The writers took advantage of these to use one as Emma's escape hatch to come and go without her parents' knowledge.
❹ All the lights are utilitarian, bare fluorescent and incandescent bulbs. ❺ We moved all the furniture and items from her upstairs bedroom as she tries to make a little oasis for herself. ❻ The floor is painted as concrete except where floor mats warm things up a little for Emma. ❼ All the brick is a plastic brick called vac form that we staple to the flats and paint to look like brick.❽ The posts jacking up the ceiling are supporting no weight. The set is built so all the walls, ceilings, and stairs can be moved when needed.

MAKEUP, HAIR, AND WARDROBE

On *Degrassi Classic*, much of the day-to-day clothes were the actors' own, but each look was created by the art department (no, Nicole Stoffman didn't dress like Stephanie Kaye in real life! But yes, that was Amanda Stepto's real hair). On *The Kids of Degrassi Street*, the young actors didn't wear makeup at all. On *Degrassi Junior High*, it was kept minimal, and on *Degrassi High*, they often did their own makeup, although the art department helped out for proper continuity.

With *Degrassi: The Next Generation*, the producers wanted to maintain the realism, while keeping in mind that modern viewing audiences expect a more polished look. But don't look for the high glamour of Hollywood. "We want you to think you could see each of those kids in your own school," explains Associate Producer Nicole Hamilton. "Wardrobe people are trained to always straighten collars, keep things crisp. They really have to fight themselves to let things be rumpled and real."

JESSICA CARTER
Key Makeup, TNG

ON MAKEUP BEYOND PRETTYING

Our department is responsible for anything on screen that's on the skin — tattoos, cuts and bruises, dirt. Craig's beating in "Going Down the Road" was a challenge. Another big challenge was the cuts on Ellie's arm. Props got the blood to "flow" (it's raspberry jam!), but we had to create the look of cuts that would gradually heal over a few episodes.

122

Amanda Milne styles
Deanna's hair.

CAITLIN

CLARA DiNUNZIO
Key Hair, TNG

ON HAIRSTYLES FOR CHARACTERS

It depends on what the actor is doing: if she's in gym class, we put her hair in a ponytail. We take our cue from wardrobe and the character. For example, if she's a sassy girl like Paige, we'll do curls and confidence. The actors are not always coiffed, like soap opera hair — some days real people's hair looks better than other days.

MELANIE JENNINGS
Costume Designer, TNG

ON THE INDIVIDUAL CHARACTERS

If there's a change for someone, I'll reflect that through the clothes. When Paige gets raped, she becomes very body conscious, so I put her in clothes that were darker and a little looser.

ON PERSONAL STYLES

Sometimes I take my cue from an actor's own personal style, if it suits the character. Adamo, for example, has a nice sense of style, so I've often reflected that in Marco. Stacey, on the other hand, couldn't be more different from how we dressed Ellie at first. As we've gotten to know Ellie, and she's found herself in better emotional shape, we've softened the look she started out with.

123

The first adventure with Stacie Mistysyn's hair was as Lisa in the episode "The Canards Move Out" on *The Kids of Degrassi Street*. When that episode was filmed, Stacie's naturally light golden brown hair was shoulder length. In editing, the producers realized another scene was needed — but Stacie had cut her hair! Luckily, the scene took place at a pool. A towel around her neck was all Stacie needed to disguise her short hair.

In the first season of *Degrassi Junior High*, Stacie's hair was short and, as Caitlin, she wore then-fashionable headbands. Not so fashionably, her headbands were made of cut-up socks! Naturally, the other sensitive young actors dubbed her "Sock head."

Art Director Judy Shiner felt that Lucy and Caitlin didn't both need to do the headband thing, and since it was working better on Lucy, Caitlin went back to normal. But not for long, as it was written into the script that, in emulation of Spike, Caitlin dyed her hair pink by day, rinsing it out before going home after school.

STACIE'S HAIR-RAISING

On the next season of DJH, Stacie got a big blonde streak in her now shoulder-length hair. Naturally, the other sensitive young actors dubbed her "Skunk." She kept this look into the first season of *Degrassi High*. Later, Caitlin was allowed a pretty normal look. She went a little blonder, and often had her hair tied back for a demure, but smart, style.

By the time she grew up, Caitlin was an elegant blonde. A successful, sophisticated reporter, her short hair reflected this when we saw her at the reunion in *The Next Generation*. When Caitlin returned as a recurring character, her blonde locks were a little longer.

Caitlin has since shown a more impulsive, fun side to her personality on TNG and so Stacie has been able to experiment with a couple of cuts and colors.

ADVENTURES

THE MUSIC OF DEGRASSI CLASSIC

WENDY WATSON and LEWIS MANNE
Music Composers and Producers

Wendy and Lewis composed, arranged, produced, and performed all the original music for *The Kids of Degrassi Street*, *Degrassi Junior High*, and *Degrassi High*. That's their voices you hear singing the theme songs.

LEWIS ON THE EVOLUTION

For *KDS*, we recorded live using a whole variety of instruments. For *DJH*, we formed a band using drums, bass, guitars, and keyboards. For dance scenes or for the music coming out of radios, we used our own song material or pre-existing songs by other Canadian recording artists.

DEGRASSI JUNIOR HIGH THEME SONG

Wake up in the morning, feeling shy and lonely.
Gee, I gotta go to this school.
I don't think I can make it, don't think I can take it,
I wonder what I'm gonna do.
But when I look around and see,
that someone is smiling right at me,
wait, someone's talkin' to me, hey, I gotta new friend.
Everybody can succeed, all you need is to believe.
Be honest with yourself, forget your fears and doubts.
Come on, give us a try at Degrassi Junior High!

DEGRASSI HIGH THEME SONG

Wake up in the morning, got to shake the feeling.
I've gotta face a day at school.
What's to be afraid of? I can ask a question,
and maybe even bend the rules.
I'm searching for a place where I fit in.
There's a way, if I look, that I can win.
Yeah, I can see I'm not alone. I can face the unknown.
Everybody can succeed, in yourself you must believe.
Give it a try at Degrassi High!

EVERYBODY WANTS SOMETHING

Everybody wants something.
They'll never give up.
Everybody wants something.
They'll take your money
and never give up.

Added lyrics for the "rock video":
Everybody get ready
and get into gear.
The Degrassi sensation,
the one and only
Zit Remedy is/The Zits are here.

Everybody face up to
the facts as they are.
Dedication is hard, but
you'll be somebody
and you will go far.

When The Zit Remedy was created, the band needed a song. Wendy and Lewis knew the words should come from the mouth of someone the age of The Zits. One weekend, their nephew, Rob, saw Lewis writing a song. A couple of weeks later, on the back of a school permission letter that never found its way to Rob's parents, the lyrics for "Everybody Wants Something" arrived in the mail.

At that time, the members of The Zit Remedy couldn't play their instruments, so every time they performed, Lewis would show up on the set, tune the guitars, and teach them how to play the notes and chords. They put their hearts into it and Lewis's biggest hit was born!

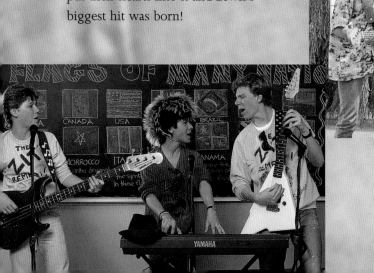

THE MUSIC OF DEGRASSI:

JODY COLERO
Music Supervisor
Jody, Jim McGrath, and Stephen Stohn composed the theme music you hear each week. Jody selects all the music for the show.

THE NEXT GENERATION THEME SONG, "WHATEVER IT TAKES"

Whatever it takes,
I know I can make it
through. (Oh yeah)
If I hold out, (If I do)
I know I can make it
through.
Be the best.
(The best I can be.
You know what
I say to you.)
Whatever it takes
(I can see it)
I know can
I can make it
(I know, I know, ahh)
I know I can make
it through.

ON THE DEGRASSI THEME

We first went with children's voices to give it that sense of joy and optimism, with a little eighties pop sound. As the kids got older, we moved to the new arrangement of the theme: heavier...and with a more mature vocal sound.

ON WHAT MUSIC DOES FOR A SCENE

It gives a scene texture and insight into a character that you don't get from just looking at the screen. Our own lives have a bit of a sound track, and that's what we do for our characters. I'm always looking for small gems of songs that perfectly reflect a moment. For instance, when Manny realizes that her choice will be to have an abortion, we have a lovely song by Lindy, called "Beautifully Undone."

ON CHOOSING THE SONGS TO USE ON THE SHOW

Almost all the songs you hear on the show are Canadian. A lot of TV shows want to sound current, so they include the latest hits from well-known artists, but we don't have that kind of budget. So we look for excellent music from artists who are not yet well-known, though some have become better known since we used their songs, such as Sam Roberts, Sloan, and Edwin. It's very important to me that I am in a position to support Canadian musicians — and that's because of how open Stephen and Linda are to that.

THE NEXT GENERATION

JIM McGRATH
Principal Composer
Jim writes the show's score and all the
background music.

ON WHETHER THAT'S REALLY THE KIDS SINGING

Absolutely. Linda really wants it to feel real, like talented kids but
not all polished — what you'd hear in high school. For technical
reasons, they're not actually playing on film, but more often than
not, if you see a character playing an instrument, it's the actor
playing that instrument on the sound track.

ON THE SOUND OF THE SHOW

I write new stuff for every scene. The pieces of the theme you hear
played on the guitar at different moments are played by David Baxter.
I play piano, organ, and other instruments. We go for a very acoustic
sound. There's a Craig and Ashley chord progression that we can play
on different instruments to create the mood that's right for the scene.

ON WHEN IT'S WORKING RIGHT

When you don't notice it. You should be wrapped up in the story,
dialogue, and emotions. Music is there to serve that. In "Time
Stands Still," we were careful not to use anything melodramatic.
We used abstract, ambient music — even no music. When Jimmy is
shot, there is no music. That's very rare in television — it really
added to the horror of the moment.

ON WORKING WITH STEPHEN STOHN

It's a delight working with a producer who's so musical himself.
Stephen is a musician who loves everything to do with sound, so
the conversation is always very meaningful.

Making music plays a big part in high school life...

It all started with The Zit Remedy. Snake first plays guitar for us in "Kiss Me Steph," when he runs for student council president: "My name is Snake — guitar, guitar — Make no mistake — guitar, guitar — To you I sez — guitar, guitar — I wanna be prez — guitar, guitar." Needless to say, he loses to "All the way with Stephanie Kaye!" By the end of the first season, the band has formed, with Joey on keyboard and Wheels on bass. At different times throughout the band's

THE GARAGE

incarnation, each of the members leaves briefly. Joey and Wheels both get grounded, and Snake takes an interest in classical guitar. Joey tries to get some air play on CRAZ (pronounced cee-are-ay-zee) Radio, and under their new name, The Zits, they manage to make a video with Lucy's help. Ultimately, the trio are friends, not bandmates.

The next generation has two musical groups that shift and change and blend. Ashley is the first musician we meet, composing the ballad "How Can I Be?" for herself and Terri — a.k.a. Two Girls and a Keyboard, or Two Girls and a Piano, as both Paige and Terri mis-state it. But when Paige gets in on the action, it's not long before they are in blue glitter, calling themselves PMS, and singing the pop-y "How

Can I B?" Same song, different beat. In "Shout, Part 2," the band (with new member Hazel) takes up the challenge of entering a girl band contest, and it's Ashley's song about rape — sung by Paige straight to Dean — that helps Paige's healing and earns them an honorable mention.

In "U Got the Look," the boys join the musical action. When Craig, Spinner, Marco, and Jimmy start their band, Joey just can't keep out of it.

"Rock and Roll High School" sets the boys against the girls — really Ashley against Craig — in a battle of the bands. With Terri in a coma, Paige and Ashley are aided by Ellie and

BANDS
OF DEGRASSI

Hazel, and are now called Hell Hath No Fury. Ashley's biting "Mr. Nice Guy" prompts Craig to write the contest-winning lyrics and apology "What I Know," performed by Downtown Sasquatch, also casually known as The Squatch.

Craig buys himself a beautiful new guitar in "Ghost in the Machine, Part 2." But with Jimmy down for the count when the band is due to use their recording studio time, Craig brings Ashley into the band — without the OK from Spinner and Marco. Sure, she's a good musician, but is she what they want? The season ends with Craig attempting to compose a song for Kevin Smith's movie. But the whole thing ends on a sour note when Skinny, the street kid, steals his beautiful, beautiful guitar...

THE MADE-UP WORLD OF DEGRASSI

The producers of *Degrassi Classic* didn't want the shows to become dated too quickly, so they avoided references to contemporary pop culture as much as possible. That's why none of the movies, TV shows, or bands are from the real world. *The Next Generation* has gone somewhat in the opposite direction, putting in some contemporary references to pop stars and pop culture. As Executive Producer Aaron Martin says, "The computers are going to date the show anyway, so it really doesn't matter." However, *TNG* still has its share of make-believe pop culture, too.

MOVIES AND TV

Melanie would have preferred to see *Crying in the Wind*, which Yick invites her to, but she can't pass up a date with Snake — even though he wants to take her to *Revenge of the Reptiles*. But Melanie does enjoy *Princes in Exile*, whose title is taken from a real movie starring Stacie Mistysyn. Stacie filmed it in Montreal while the *Degrassi High* episode "Just Friends" was being shot. Joey and Caitlin agree to disagree for a school project after they watch *Teen Academy IV*.

Degrassi characters with a romantic bent enjoy *Tender Beats the Heart* or *Return to Sender*. Yick and Arthur, on the other hand, are thwarted in their attempt to see *Swamp Sex Robots*, a video "so hot, it'll fry your eyeballs."

Even though they are on a TV show, the *Degrassi* kids don't watch much TV — but Stephanie and the twins do drool over Damon King, star of the soap opera *Days of Passion*. Apparently, there is a community-access station where Joey hopes to get The Zits' video played. The only other TV in the world of *Degrassi Classic* is the quiz show *Quest for the Best* — and the kids are on that one!

```
1 CRESTING HIMALAYA        4 6 8  AA
2 TROUBLES WITH MY UNCLE   7  9   G
3 FOR THE LOVE OF HEATHER  3 7 9  AA
4 LAKESHORE AVENUE           2 5  AA
            2 TICKET TUESDAY$
```

TNG's movie titles are also made up. Most of the movies and posters feature a star named Heather. Even some of the titles include the name Heather — *For the Love of Heather*, for example.

Marco and Dylan see the zombie movie *Killer Rage*, on their first date. *Killer Rage* is still playing the following season in "Islands in the Stream" when Paige is working her first day at the theater. When the boys arrive, they opt to see *Salvador Kovack*. Emerging from the movie, they pronounce it "surreal" and speculate as to why Kovack killed the goat.

And, of course, the biggest made-up movie of all is *Jay and Silent Bob Go Canadian, Eh?*, which is shot at Degrassi Community School and features some of the students. There's even a poster for it.

MUSIC AND RADIO

Besides The Pogues, who are real, the only bands the *Degrassi Classic* characters like are the ficticious Gourmet Scum and The Savages. The Savages even shoot a video at Degrassi High. The hit Savages' song you hear was actually written by Keith White, who played Tim on DH. Joey worked at CRAZ Radio. This is the station from which Dr. Sally broadcasts, and it is the source of the Pogues tickets Tim wins.

On *TNG*, the teens' favorite musical artist is the fictitious Kid Elrick. In "Drive," Craig, Sean, Spinner, and Marco joyride down to a promotion by Mix 99.9 — a real Toronto radio station — to win tickets to see Kid Elrick. In "Secret, Part 2," when the guys go to a concert, we get to see the Kid — sort of — for the first time.

Chapter 5

THE ISSUES

Although the *Degrassi* series have featured plenty of fun times, they have also been noted for their willingness to wade into some of the hard issues teens face every day. The shows have explored problems such as peer pressure, prejudice, body image, depression, disease, and grief. Here are a few of the many issues that *Degrassi Junior High*, *Degrassi High*, and *Degrassi: The Next Generation* have tackled.

SEXUALITY

On DJH, Caitlin has dreams about a female teacher that make her wonder whether she could be gay. Soon, rumors are flying around the school. Speaking to Ms. Avery helps Caitlin get a handle on her feelings — she's not gay, after all — but when it aired in the late 1980s, the episode struck a chord with viewers.

Years later, on TNG, the show's writers went a step further. Marco realizes that he is gay and comes out to his friends. Most of them take it well, but Spinner needs some time to accept the news. Marco's relationship with Dylan becomes strained because Marco is reluctant to come out to his parents. Even though more than a decade has passed since Caitlin's struggle with her sexual identity, the reaction to Marco's story line is as strong as ever. Viewers and parents have much to say on the issue.

Other *Degrassi* characters have to deal with the news that a family member is gay. The writers and producers wanted to portray a situation that many real-life families find themselves in every day. On DJH, Snake's older brother reveals that he is gay. Their parents ask Glen to leave and, sadly, he and

Snake eventually lose touch. On TNG, Ashley's father comes out and initially she rejects him. But by the time he marries his partner, Ashley has come to terms with the situation and even stands up for him at the wedding. No matter what the outcome, the episodes explore the issues of understanding and acceptance.

"When I saw Marco tell his mom that he was gay, I thought that took real courage and strength.... After that episode I was thinking about telling my mom I was gay. It was hard for me to tell her, but I did.... I told her and she was proud of me." — Trent S., 15

SEX...

Many characters in the *Degrassi* series deal with pressure about sex. Some close couples, like Ashley and Jimmy at the beginning of TNG, never have sex, but they still feel pressure for various reasons. Ashley backs out of sleeping with Jimmy at the last minute because she isn't actually ready, and Jimmy reveals that he isn't ready either. On DJH, Paul falsely claims he had sex with Lucy so that he'll look good to his friends. That spelled the end of their relationship.

On TNG, Emma learns the hard way that you don't have to go "all the

way" to face serious consequences about sex. She has to be treated for gonorrhea after having oral sex with Jay. Not to mention the grief she faces when word gets around at school.

... AND CONDOMS

You can't talk about sex and STDs without talking about condoms. And boy, do the *Degrassi* kids talk about condoms! From the days when *DJH*'s Joey is humiliated by a loudmouthed cashier to Jimmy's similarly uncomfortable experience with a snarky clerk on *TNG*, working up the courage to buy condoms for the first time seems to be as universally dreaded as it ever was. When it aired in Canada in 1987, the episode about Joey was thought to be possibly the first time condoms had ever been discussed on a fictional TV show. But the producers felt it was a subject that needed to be explored openly. In 2001, though, the focus was more on Jimmy's personal embarrassment than on that of society at large.

PREGNANCY

In spite of all the talk of condoms, some *Degrassi* students still make mistakes that result in accidental pregnancies. Spike is known to this day as "the girl who got pregnant" on DJH. The controversy over a fourteen-year-old going to school pregnant spilled out of the halls of *Degrassi* and into real life. Viewers, parents, and educators all made their thoughts about the Emmy-winning story line known to the producers of the show. Opinions ranged from complete outrage that such a topic had appeared in a show for young people to heartfelt gratitude that *Degrassi* had dared address the subject. However, the story line was not seen in all the countries where *Degrassi* aired — each broadcaster decided for itself whether or not to show it, and many decided not to.

Other characters made a different choice from Spike's, however, and Erica's decision to have an abortion in 1989 was just as controversial as Manny's same decision in 2004. In both cases, the episodes didn't even air in some countries, or references to the pregnancies and abortions were cut out. In Manny's case, viewers were split right down the middle. Some felt Manny should have taken

"To this day, I admire Amanda Stepto for playing the role she did when it was so very taboo...she probably helped more young girls than she could ever know!"
— Leanne B., 25

Craig's feelings about the pregnancy into account, while others thought it was ultimately her choice to make. Many viewers thought she should have considered adoption, but others thought she'd made the right decision.

ALCOHOL AND DRUGS

Both TNG and *Degrassi Classic* have dealt with the issue of alcohol abuse. Ellie and Kathleen are both alienated from their mothers because their mothers are alcoholics. Ellie goes so far as to move out of the house entirely. Alcohol has affected the *Degrassi* kids' lives in other ways, both minor and major — from Stephanie and Terri's embarrassment at school after drinking too much, to Wheels' parents being killed by a drunk driver. In spite of his parents' fate, in *School's Out!*, Wheels drives drunk and causes an accident that kills a child, permanently injures Lucy, and lands Wheels in jail. Another dose of reality from *Degrassi*: not everyone learns their lesson the first time.

The *Degrassi* kids also learn lessons about drugs, both legal and illegal. Some experiment with marijuana, like Melanie, Diana, and Kathleen on DH. Ashley does Ecstasy on *TNG*. Ritalin is a legal drug that is prescribed to Spinner, but when Jimmy takes some to enhance his on-court performance, he ends up cut from the basketball team and Spinner gets in trouble, too.

The most serious consequences of drug use are suffered by

Shane on DJH, who falls from a bridge while under the influence of acid and ends up with brain damage. Shane's story line was, unfortunately, inspired by the real life experience of a young Toronto man.

ABUSE

Abuse comes in many forms, and *Degrassi* has dealt with several of them. Craig from TNG and Rick from DJH are beaten by their fathers. Boyfriends physically abuse their girlfriends, like Terri and Kathleen — in Terri's case, with disastrous consequences. *Degrassi* has even portrayed self-abuse, as when Ellie starts cutting herself to deal with her feelings about her alcoholic mother.

Another form of abuse is bullying, which several characters on the *Degrassi* series have had to deal with. Some of these conflicts end with a truce, as in the case of Joey and Dwayne. On the other hand, some lead to a more deadly conclusion, as Rick on TNG decides to put an end to his torment by shooting his bullies, and ends up dead himself.

Sexual abuse is another topic *Degrassi* has dared to tackle. Lucy is sexually harassed by a teacher, Mr. Colby, on DJH and finally speaks up about it when she sees him advancing on Susie. On DH, Liz admits to Spike that she was sexually abused as a child by her mother's boyfriend. The story line about Paige's date rape on TNG ended with her accuser being acquitted for lack of evidence. Some viewers, although disappointed at the outcome, were appreciative of *Degrassi*'s trademark realism.

"Time Stands Still" was an episode I was really glad I saw, because it gave me kind of a second chance to think back about all the things I've said about people, and even some of my friends, that were so hurtful. — Ashley, 15

THE CAUSES

Caitlin and Emma are always trying to do their part, however small, to make the world a better place. Emma has championed endangered animals and agitated against genetically modified foods in the cafeteria. On *The Next Generation*, Caitlin is famous for her old show, *Ryan's Planet*, a natural extension of her activism against nuclear weapons and animal testing, and her promotion of Native rights. Also on *TNG*, Degrassi Community School students wore orange ribbons to protest violence against women. And who can forget the grade nine challenge at Degrassi High that ended in the toilet-papering of Mr. Raditch's yard — all in the aid of UNICEF?

The *Degrassi* series have shown that kids can make a difference. One of the longest relationships *Degrassi* has had with a cause is with UNICEF, the highly respected international development agency that protects and cares for the world's children.

Hoping one of the young actors would become the UNICEF Ontario celebrity ambassador, then Director of Communications Srinka Wallia hooked up with *Degrassi* in 1989. She got not one ambassador, but the entire repertory company! Srinka remembers: "For me, the great thing was to find young people to do a

UNICEF
RIGHTS OF THE
CHILD CAMPAIGN.
GET INVOLVED.
YOU CAN MAKE
A DIFFERENCE.

UNICEF and Special Ambassadors, the Degrassi Kids, are working for the rights of children around the world. Every kid in every country has the right to nationality, education, health care, love and under-standing and the opportunity to be the best they can be. Help us help UNICEF see that no child's rights are denied. UNICEF is making sure there is a **future for every child.**

Unicef Ontario, 325 Egerton Ave. East, Toronto, M4P 1L7 (416) 482 4444

Kids for kids

campaign for young people. Who better to get the message out?" Members of the Repco made appearances at many schools and public events, and helped promote literacy through libraries and a televised public service announcement. *The Degrassi Kids Rap on Rights*, a short video on the rights of the child, was distributed to schools across Canada.

When *Degrassi* returned to television in 2001 with a fresh new cast, Srinka saw the opportunity to renew a very successful relationship. This time, the cast members contributed prose, poetry, songs, and research that were sewn together into a more serious video called *The Global HIV/AIDS Pandemic: What are you going to do about it?* "I was blown away by the level of talent these kids have," Srinka recalls. "The singing, the playing, the writing — the ability to get a message across! I was just thinking, 'These kids are really talented and caring!'"

Visit the UNICEF Web site at www.unicef.org to find out what you can do in your country to support this cause.

Then Ontario Premier David Peterson

Chapter 6

DEGRASSI OUT THERE

An important factor in the success of *Degrassi* has been its ability to reach an audience beyond its native Canada. Not only are the various incarnations of the series broadcast all over the world, but the casts — both old and new — also took to promoting the show, and thanks to the Internet, there's a growing following in the United States and around the world.

CLASSIC PUBLICITY TOURS

One perk of being involved in a popular TV show is getting to make trips to do promotion. Cast members of the *Degrassi Classic* series were invited to make appearances across North America. At first, it was primarily this author who accompanied the young actors on trips — until she let it slip how much fun it was! Then others got a chance to get in on the fun, too!

SPREADING

When traveling by plane, one of the young actors would be in charge of checking the group through the airport and not losing the tickets — a first experience for many of them.

Everywhere the cast went, they were beautifully taken care of by their hosts, whether it was the renowned southern hospitality of Atlanta, or the unusually balmy winter weather that welcomed them to Winnipeg. The warmest welcome was in Memphis, where a group of students presented the actors with a *Degrassi* quilt they had made. The coolest welcome had to be Yellowknife, Northwest Territories, where the kids took a ride in a real dogsled reached by ski-plane, wearing parkas borrowed from Correctional Services!

Halifax was a frequent destination — the people in the streets were so friendly. Enormous turnouts in Ottawa nearly overwhelmed the kids! Hosts in Boston always planned lots of things for the kids to see and do there.

The cast returned from other destinations with great stories and adventures to recount. In London, Amanda Stepto was stopped in Covent Garden by an American tourist who wanted to be photographed with "a real English punk." When he realized she was Canadian, he laughed, and then he suddenly recognized her — he was a *Degrassi* fan!

TNG PUBLICITY TOURS

Associate Producer Nicole Hamilton has experienced the fun of accompanying the TNG kids on some of their publicity tours. In Los Angeles, when Lauren Collins popped out of the car at their hotel, Nicole heard some murmurs, which quickly became cries of, "Omigod — it's Paige!" More fans

THE WORD

suddenly seemed to appear from nowhere. Then, as Cassie emerged from the car, the screaming started. Nicole, Cassie Steele, and Lauren found themselves surrounded in their hotel lobby by fans from as far away as Oregon, clamoring for the actors' autographs and photos.

There was pandemonium at screenings in New York. "The response to the actors was insane," recalls Meeri Cunniff, producer at The N. "We saw shaking, crying, and hyperventilating." After a mall appearance, Jake Epstein and Aubrey Graham were followed on the New Jersey Turnpike by girls screaming marriage proposals from their car windows.

Nicole also accompanied Ryan Cooley and Adamo Ruggiero on another Los Angeles trip, where 2,000 fans showed up at Glendale Mall. Another 500 had to be turned away.

One appearance in Halifax with Jake Epstein "was like Beatlemania," Nicole recalls. "The crowd became a seething mass pressing closer and closer to Jake. We had to keep yelling at them to step back for their own safety. Kids were trying to climb up pillars to get a better look. And in the midst of it all, there's a sleepy, bleary-eyed Jake bewildered by it all." Remembering the scene, Nicole adds, "I don't think he understood that the mayhem was all about him — which makes him even more adorable!"

YOU SAID IT!

...I like the fact that as we get to know the [TNG] characters more, and as they grow, their problems and daily situations grow more complex, and I think that's a great thing you've done with the show. Because I used to think it was pretty simple, and now it's much more complex, and it keeps getting better every day. Count me as one of many fans of the show.
— Abigail G., 19, Monterrey, Mexico

We're maybe just a small country, but we also like Degrassi: The Next Generation very much, so that proves that you are very popular and that you have to keep up the good work! I really recognize myself in several characters, and I think many others do too.... Keep on writing new episodes!
— Iris B., Belgium

I first started watching Degrassi Junior High at the age of thirteen, and three years later I'm still obsessed with this great show. I believe the main attribute to Degrassi's success is the fact that the stories are so realistic and have happened to the majority of teenagers everywhere.... From what I have noticed, community schools in Australia and in Canada are very similar.

— Helen M., 16, Melbourne

Degrassi has taught me and my friends about Canadian culture: scary gangs from Montreal, the clothes judges wear in court, and accents.... Thank you Degrassi.

— Lane B., 13, Michigan

Degrassi. "If your life were a TV show, this would be it." The N, the U.S. nighttime network for teens, sums up this addictive show in a nutshell. Being a sixteen-year-old Degrassi fan living in the U.S., this show is a change of pace for me. It changes the outlook I have on life as a teenager. This defines real life. The characters are real. The settings are real. The situations are real. Even the theme song speaks to me.... Also I feel that the show doesn't stereotype minorities as being poor or uneducated.... Degrassi: The Next Generation has really changed my life for the better and I hope it continues to do so in the future.

— Kai C., 16, Los Angeles

DEGRASSI AROUND THE WORLD

Did you know that TNG is broadcast in these and over 100 other countries?

Australia • Belgium • Brazil • Bulgaria • Canada • Colombia • Cyprus • France • Guatemala • Indonesia • Israel • Italy • Japan • Malaysia • New Zealand • Philippines • Singapore • Spain • Sweden • United States • Venezuela

DEGRASSI ONLINE

The fans of *TNG* have a major advantage over those who watched *Degrassi Classic* in the eighties and early nineties: they have an online community where they can interact with other fans 24/7, no matter where they are in the world. Stephen Stohn and Linda Schuyler approached Raja Khanna, president of Snap Media, in 2001, about developing a Web site — even while the show itself was still in development. The goal was not only to create an interactive environment having to do with the show, but to create a place that reflects what's happening in the viewers' lives. The result was Degrassi.tv.

"It was truly a pioneering thing," Raja says. "Fortunately, we managed to excite a lot of important people with our vision for this, like the broadcaster, various funding agencies, and the government, and have had lots of support from them through it all."

Getting a Web site just right takes vision and creativity. It was Raja's idea to make the site a "virtual school." Members get "lockers" and are assigned "homerooms." Creative Developer Mark Hand developed the navigational structure. "I'm kind of an informational architect," he explains. "My job is to figure out what the 'idea' of the Web site is going to be." Site members receive "d-mail" from *TNG* characters, created by Writer Brendon

Q⁃ Google

Yorke. "People know they're fictitious," Mark acknowledges, "but they have fun suspending disbelief."

The site's moderator, Matt O'Sullivan (the same Matt O'Sullivan who creates the animation for the Web pages you see on the Media Immersion Lab's computer screens), has presided over the forums since the beginning. "It's remarkable to have been able to watch the progression of this community, and the friendships, cliques, and social groups that have developed," he says. Sort of like a school in real life!

One thing many users wonder is whether TNG's writers ever visit the site to hear what the fans are saying. "The writers love the Web site," Stephen reveals. "They actively read the postings...not for story ideas, but for the way kids are talking about things, what's of interest to them, and the language they use, to help them write the dialogue for the show." So, yes, they're listening. Be sure to make yourself heard!

Stephen is justifiably proud of the Web site's success. "There are about 125,000 people who visit the site regularly, and over 600,000 people are registered." Degrassi.tv is said to be the most successful Web site for a television drama in the world!

THE DOT

Ever wonder where the kids' hangout, The Dot, got its name? Well, Matt knows:

"Sometime near the beginning of the site, [member] LittleOzzy made a post where the subject line was simply '.' — that was it, no real topic! Well, that post is still there today, and has over 30,000 messages posted to it! It's a virtual clubhouse, and it just keeps going and going. It's not about anything, and that was the point, I guess. Just a place to hang out. And that's why the name of the hangout on the show is The Dot."

Chapter 7

PARTY!

Whether it's *Degrassi Classic* or *TNG*, the kids — and adults — are always up for a party. Unfortunately, most of these parties are doomed to failure. But don't be afraid: follow the Queen's University Degrassi Club's example and plan your own *Degrassi* party. You'll see that the creative team and actors have had much better luck at their own celebrations — whether it's wrapping up the end of another successful season or toasting the awards and accolades they have received.

THROW A DEGRASSI PARTY

A few freshmen at Queen's University in Kingston, Ontario discovered their shared love of *Degrassi* in the common room of their dorm. Later, they went to the *Jonovision Degrassi* reunion taping together. Soon, they'd decided to make it official. The response was huge on Clubs Night at Queen's the next year. Club events included a visit from Queen's Film Studies professor and former DJH director Clarke Mackey and a *Degrassi* party. The Queen's Degrassi Club is still active, despite founder Mark Janson having graduated in 2003. Mark describes how

A *Degrassi* party about to go wrong

the hugely successful party was planned and executed. Use this as a guide for a *Degrassi* party of your own! You can keep it old school (*Degrassi Classic*) or go totally new school (TNG) — the choice is yours.

MARK JANSON
Queen's Degrassi Club Founder

ON HOW THE PARTY WAS PLANNED

We all drew names to decide who was going to be which character. Everybody went all-out with their costumes. We got all kinds of eighties music, particularly anything to do with *Degrassi* — The Pogues, Gowan's "Moonlight Desires," and of course a few Zit Remedy tracks as well. As for food, we just went with a bunch of potato chips — an eighties classic.

ON HOW THINGS WENT DOWN

The girl who was "Lucy" came over early to welcome everyone because, technically, it was her party — who else threw parties at Degrassi besides Lucy? That is how we pitched the invitations as well, along the line of Lucy's parents being out of town. On top of this, we had some *Degrassi* episodes going on a few different TVs too, which was cool.

ON THE VIBE

Overall, it felt like one of the *Degrassi* parties you'd see on TV, only with more alcohol (we were legal drinking age, after all). The funny thing was that everyone hung out with the person their character would have hung out with. "Yick" and "Arthur" just naturally drifted together, for instance!

ON HINDSIGHT BEING 20/20

In retrospect, it would have been a good idea to have arranged for someone playing Diana's older brother to come in and bust up the party....

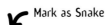 Mark as Snake

CELEBRATION TIME

One of the perks of working on *Degrassi* is the fantastic parties you get to go to! Check out the past and present cast and executive celebrating at award galas, screenings, and wrap parties.

AWARDS

Degrassi has been nominated for and won so many awards, it would be impossible to list them all here! Instead, here are just a few of the highlights from the series' twenty-five-year history.

2004
Gemini Awards
- Best Children's or Youth Fiction Program or Series
- Best Direction in a Children's or Youth Program or Series: Philip Earnshaw, "Pride"

2003
Gemini Awards
- Best Children's or Youth Fiction Program or Series
- Best Direction in a Children's or Youth Program or Series: Bruce McDonald, "Weird Science"
- Best Performance in a Children's or Youth Program or Series: Jake Epstein, "Tears Are Not Enough"

Directors Guild of Canada Awards
- Outstanding Achievement in a Television Series — Children's: Bruce McDonald and team, "When Doves Cry"
- Outstanding Achievement in Direction — Television Series: Bruce McDonald, "White Wedding"

- Outstanding Achievement in Picture Editing — Short Form: Stephen Withrow, "White Wedding"

2002
Directors Guild of Canada Awards
- Outstanding Achievement in a Television Series — Children's: Bruce McDonald, "Mother and Child Reunion"

Young Artist Awards
- Best Ensemble in a Television Series

1992
Prix Jeunesse International
- *Degrassi High*, "Bad Blood"

1991
Parents' Choice Awards
- *Degrassi High*

1989
Gemini Awards
- Best Dramatic Series: *Degrassi Junior High*
- Best Performance by an Actress in a Leading Role: Stacie Mistysyn

Parents' Choice Awards

- *Degrassi Junior High*

1988
Gemini Awards

- Best Continuing Dramatic Series:
  Degrassi Junior High
- Best Direction in a Dramatic or Comedy
  Series: Kit Hood
- Best Performance by an Actor in a
  Leading Role: Pat Mastroianni
- Multiculturalism Gemini

Parents' Choice Awards

- *Degrassi Junior High*

1987
Canadian Film and Television Awards

- Personal Achievement: Kit Hood and
  Linda Schuyler

Gemini Awards

- Best Children's Program: *Degrassi Junior High*
- Best Direction in a Dramatic or
  Comedy Series: Kit Hood

International Emmy Awards

- Children & Young People:
  Degrassi Junior High, "It's Late"

1986
Gemini Awards

- Best Children's Program:
  The Kids of Degrassi Street

International Emmy Awards

- Children & Young People: *The Kids of
  Degrassi Street*, "Griff Gets a Hand"

Prix Jeunesse International

- *The Kids of Degrassi Street*,
  "Griff Makes a Date"

Chapter 8

THE EPISODES

The Kids of Degrassi Street started out

with just one half-hour film and blossomed to twenty-six episodes about kids' everyday lives in Toronto's East End, locale of the real Degrassi Street. The episodes make sense if watched separately, but the same characters reappear in different episodes.

IDA MAKES A MOVIE
Ida's movie is chosen for an award, but for the wrong reasons! Should she tell the judges or not?

COOKIE GOES TO HOSPITAL
Ida's best friend, Cookie, is in hospital and she *needs* her doll. For Ida, to visit that "creepy" place is a real test of loyalty.

IRENE MOVES IN
New girl, Irene, and Cookie are getting along just a little too well for Ida's taste. And Bigfoot has been spotted in the area!

LISA MAKES THE HEADLINES

Lisa needs a big scoop to get the neighborhood interested in her newspaper. But what happens when reporting the scoop means telling on her own brother?

NOEL BUYS A SUIT

Noel's dad is remarrying and Gayle is taking over *everything* — including deciding what Noel will wear to the wedding.

SOPHIE MINDS THE STORE

Chuck's offer to help Sophie mind her family's store backfires when Sophie finds the day's receipts $20 short. The thief must be Chuck, right?

BILLY BREAKS THE CHAIN

Billy knows it's hard work, not luck, that will get him into hockey camp. But disasters begin to occur when he hesitates about passing on a bad-luck chain letter.

CASEY DRAWS THE LINE

A new survey line goes right through the pen of the rabbit Lisa and Casey share. So whose responsibility is Rabbit now?

PETE TAKES A CHANCE

Pete's latest money-making scheme is a surefire winner. But his "investment" costs him more than he expected when he puts his friendships on the line.

CHUCK MAKES A CHOICE

Is Chuck's dad an airline pilot, or is he serving time? With the school play coming up, the secret is bound to come out.

CATHERINE FINDS HER BALANCE

When both her divorced parents want to come and watch her at the gymnastics meet, Catherine, a.k.a. Cookie, works quite the balancing act to prevent a scene.

BENJAMIN WALKS THE DOG

Billy and Pete will do anything to get rid of Billy's pesky little brother — until it looks like they've gotten rid of him forever.

LIZ SITS THE SCHLEGELS

Liz finds she has her hands full when she takes on a babysitting job with two lively kids and one who refuses to have anything to do with her.

THE CANARDS MOVE OUT

Lisa doesn't want to leave Degrassi Street and move to Vancouver. But it seems no one will listen to her feelings on the subject.

MARTIN MEETS THE PIRATES

While Martin wrestles with his conscience over whether to join the Pirates, Pete tries in vain to rally the neighborhood to protect Degrassi Street from the gang.

CONNIE GOES TO COURT

Connie isn't worried that she can't pay the five dollars she owes. She'll pay after she goes collecting for her paper route. But then the paper goes on strike!

RACHEL RUNS FOR OFFICE

Rachel's a serious candidate, while Billy is pulling ahead on a frivolous campaign. Rachel learns something that is sure to win her the election — but is it fair to use it?

GRIFF MAKES A DATE

Hooray! Lisa's back from Vancouver! On the serious side, she has just learned her baby brother is mentally challenged. When new kid Griff calls the crossing guard a retard, he finds he may have lost his first friend.

SAMANTHA GETS A VISITOR

Samantha and her cousin Lisa, from the big city, have started to grow apart. But a night lost in the woods puts things back into perspective.

JEFFREY FINDS A FRIEND

Jeffrey bets Connie that he will do better than she will on the next math test. So when Griff arrives looking for last-minute help, Jeffrey must decide — study what he needs to, or help his new friend?

CONNIE MAKES A CATCH

Connie tries to attract the popular captain of the baseball team, but it isn't easy for a tomboy to act like a lady. Lisa has the opposite problem — Griff wants to take her to the movies, but her parents have said no.

KAREN KEEPS HER WORD

Karen can think about nothing but the roller skates she wants, until she learns the hard way the importance of a commitment — to a cause, or to a friend.

RYAN RUNS FOR HELP

Ryan loves to be the center of attention. But when his tales of buried treasure lead Benjamin to fall into a hole on a construction site, it seems his attention-getting abilities have worn out.

MARTIN HEARS THE MUSIC

The Talent Show is coming, but Rachel, the only one with any talent, refuses to go on. Martin won't wear his hearing aid and may also quit.

LISA GETS THE PICTURE

Tension comes between best friends Casey and Lisa when Lisa starts spending just a bit too much time with Griff. Is Lisa being selfish, or is Casey just jealous?

GRIFF GETS A HAND

When Griff's friend Danny the crossing guard dies of a stroke, Griff just gives up. What's the point of anything, even Lisa and his grade six year?

With **Degrassi Junior High**, the number of episodes per season jumped to thirteen. Although the episodes can stand alone, characters begin to have story arcs that span whole seasons, and incidents that take place in some episodes reverberate throughout the series. Several actors from **The Kids of Degrassi Street** moved on to **Degrassi Junior High**, and new character names and circumstances were created for them.

KISS ME, STEPH

Voula is aghast when her best friend, Stephanie, begins campaigning for president on kisses and wild promises. Meanwhile, Stephanie's kid brother, Arthur, joins forces with Yick to avoid Joey's bullying.

THE BIG DANCE

Voula disagrees with her father that she is too young to go to the dance and slips out anyway. Her plan goes awry when she is asked to make the speech that Stephanie, the school president, is too drunk to make.

THE EXPERIMENT

Yick, convinced Mr. Raditch is picking on him, sets up an experiment, handing in as his own an old paper of Stephanie's. Joey finds himself in hot water when Kathleen and Melanie believe the vitamin pills he has sold them are really drugs.

THE COVER UP

Joey is fascinated by Rick, the school tough guy, but when he goes to Rick's place after school, he finds out that his bruises aren't from street fights, but inflicted by Rick's own father. Caitlin and Susie try to make Rick smile.

THE GREAT RACE

The girls' swim team has been challenged to a battle of the sexes swimming race by the boys' soccer team. Yick and Arthur have their own problems — it seems like everyone's had a growth spurt but them.

RUMOR HAS IT

Rumors are flying that Ms. Avery is gay. When Caitlin starts dreaming about her favorite teacher, she begins to wonder about her own sexuality. Rick goes on a spending spree after $20 disappears from Yick's locker.

THE BEST LAID PLANS

Stephanie asks Wheels out on a date, but bravado and misunderstandings lead both to imply to their friends that they'll do something neither is ready for. Yick has pinched a video from his brother — *Swamp Sex Robots* is so hot it'll fry your eyeballs!

NOTHING TO FEAR

When L.D.'s dad goes into hospital, she is so paralyzed with fear that she lets down her family and her friends. Amadeus, the school's snake, gets loose and Melanie just knows she'll be the one to find it unexpectedly.

WHAT A NIGHT!

Voula goes shopping with Lucy, but when she finds out Lucy doesn't pay for her purchases, it's too late — the police have already been called. When Stephanie meets her soap opera star idol, she can hardly believe her luck.

SMOKE SCREEN

Rick takes an interest in the Environmental Action Committee and Caitlin decides he can be redeemed if people will give him a chance. Arthur accidentally breaks what he believes is Yick's family heirloom vase.

IT'S LATE

When Spike's period is late, she can hardly believe it — she never meant to go as far as she did with Shane. Yick has a crush on Melanie, and seeks Arthur's romantic advice, since Yick's never asked a girl out on a date before.

PARENTS' NIGHT

When Wheels' birth father shows up out of the blue, Wheels has to deal with his feelings about his adoptive parents, his birth parents, and who he really is. Spike asks Wheels for advice on whether to put her baby up for adoption.

REVOLUTION!

To make Wheels jealous, Stephanie puts Joey into the vacant post of sports rep, though a grade seven student normally holds the position. The grade seven class moves to impeach her, but Arthur is torn — does he side with his class or his sister?

SEASON 2 picks up where Season 1 left off, portraying the second semester of junior high, although it was filmed the subsequent year. In Canada, in 1988, the second season began its Monday at 8:30 p.m. run, which was to remain the time slot for the rest of the shows. Across the United States, PBS stations began airing the series in various time slots.

EGGBERT

When Shane says he wants to help Spike, "Eggbert" — an egg that represents a baby — becomes his responsibility. Stephanie decides to change her image and gives all her sexy clothes to Alexa.

A HELPING HAND

Lucy has finally found a teacher who appreciates her. L.D. is just being silly when she claims Mr. Colby appreciates Lucy a little too much — isn't she? Wheels has to take extra tutoring after school and can't practice with The Zit Remedy.

GREAT EXPECTATIONS

Liz, the new girl, looks to Joey like the type who will "do it," and it's pretty obvious she likes him. Yick urges Arthur to phone "Talking Sex with Dr. Sally" to find out the truth about the strange, "leaky" dreams he's been having.

DINNER AND A SHOW

Shane is trying to do the right thing by Spike and the baby, but his parents want to send him off to private school. Melanie has a date with Yick, but when Snake invites her out on the same night, she can't pass up the opportunity.

STAGE FRIGHT

Caitlin is determined that having epilepsy isn't going to make any difference in her life, and she resolves to get the lead in the school play. Michelle is paralyzed at the thought of having to make a speech in class.

FIGHT!

Dwayne challenges Joey to a fight. Joey tries everything, but it looks like there's no way to get out of a sound thrashing. Stephanie, back in her sexy clothes, is sure she's come up with a way to get Simon to notice her.

BOTTLED UP

Kathleen has made the quiz-show team! When the team comes to her house to practice, the worst happens — her mother comes into the room, drunk as usual. Max and Scooter decide it's time to start being cool — just like Rick.

SEALED WITH A KISS

Erica wants to grow up and be her own person. But after kissing a boy she hardly knows, she gets sick. Heather sees a way to get back at her sister. Now that Wheels is back in The Zit Remedy, Snake seems to be ducking rehearsals.

DOG DAYS

Arthur and Stephanie's mother announces she's remarrying, and she expects Arthur to come and live with them. Stephanie's near the end of her rope — she's had enough go wrong lately without this, too.

CENSORED

It looks like Spike is going to be thrown out of Degrassi. Caitlin is horrified and decides to use the newspaper to champion Spike's cause. L.D. starts a campaign to stop the boys from putting pictures of bikini-clad girls in their lockers.

TRUST ME

Snake's parents go away for the weekend, so Joey invites himself and Wheels to stay over and borrow Snake's parents' car for a little joyriding. The twins are upset when it looks like Spike will be thrown out of Degrassi after all.

HE'S BACK...

Lucy's worst nightmare comes true when Mr. Colby returns. She sees him being extra friendly to Susie and realizes something has to be done. Alex, school treasurer, desperately tries to think up a way to raise enough money to finish the yearbook.

PASS TENSE

Wheels is not sure he's going to pass. Joey just laughs at him — but he never has to work for his marks. Spike has missed so much school that she might fail. The school board is adding grade nine to Degrassi. It's just not fair!

In **SEASON 3**, to keep the characters together, the producers decided that Degrassi Junior High would now have a grade nine. The grade nines would be bused to a nearby high school for certain classes, which provided the opportunity to introduce some new, older characters to the mix. New grade sevens arrive at Degrassi, too. The season expands to fifteen half-hour episodes.

CAN'T LIVE WITH 'EM

This is *Degrassi Junior High*'s first one-hour special. Joey is stuck in grade eight; Arthur's mother has won the lottery; the grade nines are finding out about high school, if only part time; and strange little kids have arrived at Degrassi, including Arthur's cousin Dorothy. Wheels is having a tough time with his parents, but not nearly as tough a time as he's about to have — after they are killed by a drunk driver.

A BIG GIRL NOW

Lucy's got a boyfriend! She doesn't have quite as much time for L.D., and Paul has "expectations," but she can handle it. Snake deals with Wheels' parents' death. Kathleen is obnoxious about her candidacy for president.

SEASONS GREETINGS

It's boiling in the cafeteria as the school's furnace goes crazy. And long-time friends Yick and Arthur are fighting. Dorothy does her best to patch it up — after all, "It's Christmas!" Spike has an unexpected visitor at school.

LOVES ME, LOVES ME NOT

Caitlin likes Joey, and he could use all the help he can get to pass grade eight. It's perfect when the two are paired up in class. Alexa helps Michelle get to know B.L.T. Dorothy has a crush on Yick.

HE AIN'T HEAVY

When Snake's brother, Glen, comes home unexpectedly from med school, it is to tell the family that he's gay. Snake isn't sure he can handle it. Joey continues his quest for fame in the music business and lands a job at CRAZ Radio.

THE WHOLE TRUTH

When Liz brings up the issue of animal rights, Caitlin leaps in with both feet. Bartholemew and Scooter order sea creatures from the back of a comic book. Joey's job at CRAZ is not all he hoped it would be.

STAR-CROSSED

Erica likes Clutch, but he invites her twin sister, Heather, to the bowling tournament. No problem, that's the joy of being twins — they'll just switch. Things are not working out between Alexa and B.L.T., and she's decided she wants Simon back.

FOOD FOR THOUGHT

Kathleen is so irritable, Melanie is going to kill her before the Science Fair is over. Of course, Kathleen is moody because she never eats. Erica and Heather are working on a project on eating disorders and worry about Lucy.

TWENTY BUCKS

Melanie's wish comes true when Snake invites her to a concert, dutch. But her mom won't give her the money — not voluntarily, anyway. Joey makes a bet that he can get a date for Friday night. The tension gets worse between Shane and Spike.

TAKING OFF, PART 1

Wheels' grandmother is talking about putting him in a group home. Shane looks forward to the Gourmet Scum concert. It's going to be extra special because Luke knows where they can score some acid.

TAKING OFF, PART 2

After Wheels' birth father sends a postcard from Port Hope, he hitchhikes to find him, but things don't turn out as he expected. Shane is missing after the concert and the police find him lying hurt under a bridge.

MAKING WHOOPEE

Arthur enjoys the bachelor life with his dad, but now his dad's girlfriend seems to be around all the time — she even comes to Open House! Melanie notices that Snake has another admirer: that pretty girl, Alison.

BLACK AND WHITE

Michelle and B.L.T. are getting along great. But when he walks her home one evening, her parents aren't so happy about her date. Could it be because he's black and she's white? Spike's daycare falls through, and she has to find a job.

PA-ARTY!

Lucy's parents are away — party! This one's going to be a blast, with some high school kids coming. Joey tries to liven up the party by supplying the beer. The police, however, have other ideas.

BYE-BYE JUNIOR HIGH

The grade nines are going on to high school next year, and the grade eights will be kings of the school. Wheels can't see how he'll pass, and Spike has some tough choices to make. It's the graduation dance, but they never got that old boiler working, and Scooter thinks he smells smoke....

Degrassi High is a direct continuation of **Degrassi Junior High**. As the actors grow up, the characters all move on to high school. The original grade eights are now in grade ten and continue on to grade eleven in the second season of **Degrassi High**. The original grade sevens are now in grade nine. Although there are a few characters who should now be in grade eight, they must have been a particularly smart bunch, as they've all managed to make it into grade nine, too. (Shh! You're not supposed to notice!)

A NEW START
This hour-long special explores what happens when a teenager's code of ethics comes into conflict with a practical reality. When Erica misses her period after a summer

fling, she fears she may be pregnant. She doesn't want to have a baby, but she is opposed to abortion. Joey meets his old nemesis, Dwayne, who decides to bring back outlawed initiation — especially for Joey, Snake, and Wheels. Simon's newfound celebrity as poster boy for Dude Jeans causes trouble for his girlfriend Alexa.

BREAKING UP IS HARD TO DO
Michelle's parents split, and she is forced to choose between them, but neither choice seems right. She only has B.L.T. to turn to, but is forbidden to see him. Erica faces a hate campaign. The Zits enlist Lucy's help to make a video.

DREAM ON

Arthur develops a crush on Caitlin. He dreams of romance and candlelit dinners — how come he's always interrupted just when he gets to the good part? It looks like it might finally be Kathleen's turn for romance, too. And the guy is in at least grade eleven!

EVERYBODY WANTS SOMETHING

Lucy agrees to shoot The Zits' video — if they can agree on a script and persuade Clutch to lend them his car. Joey plans to deal with Caitlin just as soon as the video's done. The hate campaign against Erica escalates.

NOBODY'S PERFECT

Kathleen's dreams are coming true. Scott is perfect — considerate, affectionate, and even gives her flowers. She can forgive him if he's hot-tempered. Liz encourages Spike to date for the first time since Emma was born.

JUST FRIENDS

Heather thinks Wheels is cute and throws a party thinking everything will fall into place. The girls go to a movie, but don't invite Maya because of her wheelchair. Lucy learns that L.D. has cancer.

LITTLE WHITE LIES

Diana is determined to grow up, but her older brother is old-fashioned. But Yick is going to be at Melanie's party. How will Diana's brother ever know she went? Joey, Snake, and Wheels decide it's time they went to a strip show.

SIXTEEN, PART 1

Michelle finds her father impossible to live with. Now that she's sixteen she can legally move out, if only she had the money. Of course, there is that family ring she got for her birthday. Joey and Snake are excited about starting driving lessons.

SIXTEEN, PART 2

Living on her own proves more of a challenge than Michelle expected. Spike is nervous about how fond Patrick is becoming of her. Alexa's birthday plans take an unexpected turn when her cake becomes L.D.'s.

ALL IN A GOOD CAUSE

Caitlin and Claude want to protest against a factory that's involved with nuclear missiles. The grade nines are competing to raise money for UNICEF, but it looks like Arthur and the gang are going to lose and become the slaves of 9B for a week.

NATURAL ATTRACTIONS

Erica starts seeing a new boy, and Heather must come to terms with having supported Erica's abortion. Alison gives up on her campaign to win Snake, but when he invites Amy to the dance, the claws come out. Scooter notices that his pal Tessa is (gasp!) a girl!

TESTING 1...2...3

Joey's school problems have not let up, so he figures if he's going to be a moron, he might as well drop out. Caitlin is terrified about her upcoming court date and Claude is no help at all. Yankou gets hold of last year's science exam.

IT CREEPS!

Lucy writes and directs her first film. But her feminist horror flick doesn't turn out quite the way she expected. Spike is nervous when Shane starts hanging around the school.

STRESSED OUT

Caitlin is devastated when Ms. Avery decides to quit teaching. Michelle starts taking caffeine pills to extend her study time. Snake suffers from a mysterious ailment that won't go away.

SEASON 2
Playing With Time decided that this season would be the show's last. The story ends with the students being split up and sent to various local schools for their final years, as Degrassi High School is to be completely renovated.

BAD BLOOD, PART 1
Joey is raising money for a muscle car and takes bets that he will walk through the cafeteria wearing nothing but a hat! Dwayne receives a frightening phone call from his summer girlfriend. B.L.T. has trouble breaking up with Michelle.

BAD BLOOD, PART 2
Joey and Dwayne's enmity escalates when Joey finds out who turned him in for the cafeteria stunt. Dwayne becomes increasingly withdrawn as he awaits the results of his HIV test. Michelle finds out the real reason B.L.T. broke up with her.

LOYALTIES
Michelle, B.L.T., Simon, and Alexa were once the fabulous four, but now that Michelle and B.L.T. have split, Alexa's loyalties are divided. Snake has a crush on Michelle. Caitlin discovers her father is seeing another woman.

A TANGLED WEB
Wheels' lies to his grandmother become more elaborate, and when he's grounded for his marks, Wheels concocts another story so he can go to a concert. Caitlin is upset about her father's infidelity. Yankou doesn't know what to do about his crush on Tessa.

BODY POLITICS

The girls' volleyball team is upset that the boys' basketball team is getting preferential treatment. Lucy is set to fight, until she discovers that Dale is the captain. Spike is jealous when Patrick invites Liz out. Alexa tries to make up with Michelle.

CROSSED WIRES

Tim's attempt to kiss Liz goodnight reawakens her memories of sexual abuse. Yankou wants to kiss Tessa, but he's not sure whether she wants him to. Joey feels pressured with Wheels living in his house. Dwayne's friends don't know what's bothering him.

THE ALL-NIGHTER

Diana's birthday sleepover at Melanie's holds more than one surprise when Kathleen finds some marijuana. Yick persuades Luke to invite Arthur to a poker game. Yankou pulls an all-nighter to get an assignment done on time.

HOME SWEET HOME

Wheels wears out his welcome at Joey's house when he steals money from Mrs. Jeremiah. Where will he sleep? Michelle, worn down by work, school, and roommates, considers moving back home.

EXTRACURRICULAR ACTIVITIES

Lucy and the twins hear The Savages are making a video at the school and decide to sneak in to see them. Joey and Snake also discover the band is at Degrassi. Caitlin's parents ask her to come home to talk.

SHOW TIME, PART 1

Talent Night auditions are on. Joey is struggling in science. Alexa is thinking of breaking up with Simon. The whole school is thrown into turmoil when a student commits suicide at school — especially Caitlin, since the student is Claude.

SHOW TIME, PART 2

Should the gang go
through with Talent
Night? Snake must deal
with his discovery of
Claude's body. Joey still
needs help with science,
and Mr. Webster has set
him up with a tutor —
Caitlin, who is still
suffering from the effects
of Claude's suicide.

THREE'S A CROWD

Spike invites Snake to the
graduation semi-formal,
but then Michelle invites
him, and he'd really
rather go with her. Tessa
is becoming bored with
Yankou, but she doesn't
want to hurt his feelings.
Amy and Alison are
desperate for dates to the
semi-formal.

ONE LAST DANCE

Dwayne deals with his
feelings about being HIV-
positive and with others'
reactions. Lucy runs for
school president. Joey
wants to ask Caitlin to
the semi-formal — which
takes on new significance
when it comes out that
it's not just the year's
last dance. It's Degrassi's
last dance.

SCHOOL'S OUT!

Although the Degrassi student body was scattered to a number of schools for the original grade eights' final year of high school, the gang kept in touch, and have a final summer together before moving on to work, school, marriage, and travel.

Joey is in love with Caitlin, but she's not ready to give up her virginity. On the other hand, Tessa seems more than willing! Wheels is working as a mechanic and enjoys a few beers now and then. Lifeguard Snake is just waiting for his chance to rescue a beautiful girl.

Relationships are tested at the end of summer when the gang goes to the cottage. Caitlin learns the truth about Joey and Tessa. Snake puts his rescue skills to the test. Scariest of all, after a few beers, Wheels drives Lucy into town for chips. It's the end of Lucy's glittering future, Wheels' freedom, and the life of an innocent child.

Simon and Alexa's autumn wedding reunites many Degrassi young adults, and they all realize that forward is the only way they can go.

the producers decided to turn the cameras in a different direction. Some of the actors from **Degrassi** served as hosts for the **Degrassi Talks** series that looked at many of the issues explored on the show, as they affected real-life members of the audience.

SEX

Amanda Stepto (Spike) hosts a look at the stories of teenagers who have been forced to make difficult decisions regarding the consequences of sexual activity. We learn about young people who have faced pregnancy, parenthood, STDs including AIDS, and infertility.

ALCOHOL

Traveling across the country with host Neil Hope (Wheels), we witness the devastating effects of drinking and driving from both the victim's and the driver's point of view and hear from other young Canadians who are dealing with the effects of alcohol.

ABUSE

With Rebecca Haines (Kathleen), we meet young adults who have been victims of some form of abuse: emotional, physical, and sexual. We also meet a young perpetrator. The interviewees offer hope that there is life after sexual assault and other abuse.

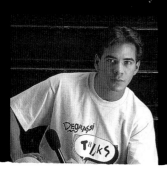

DEPRESSION

Pat Mastroianni (Joey) introduces us to teens who are overwhelmed with feelings of apathy in a society that is filled with environmental destruction, peer pressure, and alienation, and yet manage to speak openly of their fears and hopes.

DRUGS

Host Siluck Saysanasy (Yick) brings us to teens who have been hit the hardest by drug use to see how their abuse has led to the destruction of the family unit and even to jail. A reformed solvent abuser talks about the particular drug problem in native communities.

SEXUALITY

Stacie Mistysyn (Caitlin) talks to a young gay man and lesbian woman about the difficulties of "coming out" in high school. We also hear about first loves, first sexual encounters, and the experiences and excitement of becoming an adult.

After the closing notes of **School's Out!** faded from the airwaves, **Degrassi** fans contented themselves with several runs of repeats. New fans who were too young to have seen the shows in their original broadcasts emerged, just as captivated by the adventures and dilemmas faced by the gang as the original viewers had been. When **Degrassi**'s creators figured out that Emma, Spike's baby from the classic series, would be entering junior high soon, **Degrassi: The Next Generation** was born.

MOTHER AND CHILD REUNION

A one-hour special kicks off the new series. After months of flirting via e-mail, twelve-year-old Emma's new love interest, Jordan, is going to be in town. With her mom and the other grown-ups at their ten-year high school reunion, Emma decides to go and meet Jordan without telling a soul, not even her friends. Meanwhile, at the reunion, old friends from Degrassi are catching up and rekindling old flames.

FAMILY POLITICS

Ashley is running unopposed for school president. Toby, spurred on by his and Ashley's awkward new situation as stepsiblings, convinces J.T. to run against her. The conflict follows Toby and Ashley home.

EYE OF THE BEHOLDER

Terri, feeling unattractive, wants to skip the school dance, but lets Ashley and Paige make her over when Spinner seems interested. Paige wants Spinner for herself and gets Terri embarrassingly drunk.

PARENTS' DAY

Toby is worried about Parents' Day — the last time his divorced parents were in the same room they had a huge, mortifying fight. He plans to keep them apart but it all comes apart on him — with positive results!

THE MATING GAME

Ashley and Jimmy's eight-month anniversary is coming up — and so is the question of whether to have sex. Paige plants doubts in Ashley's mind. If Ash doesn't "put out" soon, will Jimmy move on?

BASKETBALL DIARIES

Jimmy wants to make the basketball team and convinces hyperactive Spinner to skip a Ritalin pill and give it to him instead, with disastrous results. Liberty wants to read the announcements.

SECRETS AND LIES

Ashley's dad is back in town with a secret that must come out — he's gay. Ashley has trouble accepting that fact. J.T. resorts to extreme measures to put an end to Liberty's crush.

COMING OF AGE

Jimmy has pretty much adopted Ashley's family and Ashley is feeling way too crowded. Should she dump him? Emma gets her first period — in a white skirt! — on presentation day!

RUMORS AND REPUTATION

Liberty is spending an awful lot of alone time with Mr. Armstrong. It's not long before rumors start to fly. Spinner plots his revenge on the cafeteria for lousy food, but he's the one who gets bitten.

FRIDAY NIGHT

When is a date not a date? When Emma's not sure if Sean really meant to ask her out. To get back at "The Wrath of Kwan," Spinner and Jimmy play a series of tricks on their least favorite teacher.

WANNABE

Paige starts a "spirit squad" at Degrassi, and Manny wants to show off her gymnastic skills and join. Emma is aghast at the reappearance of the sexist tradition. J.T and Toby think they have won one million dollars.

CABARET

Ashley is convinced her beautiful ballad will make her and Terri stars of the cabaret, but Paige wants to join and add some sparkle. Toby will do anything to get on Emma's good side — including donning tights.

UNDER PRESSURE

Faced with the pressure of passing grade seven, Sean slips into old, angry patterns and picks a fight with Jimmy. He passes the exam, but loses Emma. Spinner fakes sick to get out of a test.

JAGGED LITTLE PILL

With their parents away for the weekend, Ashley decides to join Toby in breaking the "one-guest-each" rule. Sean confiscates Toby and J.T.'s Ecstasy and Ashley takes it. Disaster piles upon disaster for Ashley.

SEASON 2

WHEN DOVES CRY: A DEGRASSI SPECIAL

Craig's father forbids him to make contact with Joey and Angela, but Craig can't seem to stop himself, even if his father's rages leave him bruised. His dad gives him money for the camera he broke, but Craig uses the money to run off. Paige agrees to a date with J.T. — for $30.

GIRLS JUST WANNA HAVE FUN

When Spike reveals she's been dating Mr. Simpson (Snake), Emma is shocked — he's her teacher! When Spike bails on Emma to go out with Snake, Emma rebels. Jimmy and Spinner challenge each other in break-dancing.

KARMA CHAMELEON

Nobody's willing to forget how Ashley treated them at her party, but when she apologizes to everyone, it's all OK — at first. Toby has a crush on Kendra and finds out her big brother is — gulp! — Spinner.

WEIRD SCIENCE

Emma's a contender at the Science Fair, until the results of her experiment don't fit her hypothesis. Spinner learns he should not wear track pants.

DRIVE

Joey goes away for the weekend and Craig is allowed to have the guys over! What harm could borrowing a car off Joey's lot do? Ellie takes Ashley to get her belly button pierced.

SHOUT, PART 1

Dean, a soccer player from Bardell, invites Paige to a house party. Ducking Spinner, she ends up in an upstairs room with Dean, and he won't take no for an answer.

IN TRIBUTE TO **DEGRASSI CLASSIC**, ALL TITLES FROM SEASON 2 ONWARD ARE TAKEN FROM THE NAMES OF EIGHTIES SONGS.

SHOUT, PART 2

Desperately trying to appear normal, Paige tries to distract herself with a girl band contest. When Ash shows up with a new song about rape, Paige reveals her secret. J.T. and Toby have trouble as locker mates.

MIRROR IN THE BATHROOM

Toby decides to join the wrestling team and, to make the lowest weight class, he sneaks laxatives and runs endless training sessions. Terri has trouble with her new fame as a plus-size model.

TAKE MY BREATH AWAY

Manny has a huge crush on Craig and actually asks him out. After their date, Craig has to figure out how to let Manny down easy. Liberty's foray into being a "bad girl" has bad consequences.

DON'T BELIEVE THE HYPE

It's International Day and Hazel is acting mean to Fareeza, a Muslim girl. When Fareeza's display on Iraq is vandalized, Hazel confesses that she's not Jamaican as she has pretended, but Somali and Muslim.

WHITE WEDDING: A DEGRASSI SPECIAL

When Spike discovers she's pregnant days before her wedding to Snake, she can't figure out how — or even if — she'll tell him. Emma's beside herself when she finds out her mom is thinking of an abortion or even calling off the wedding. J.T. and Toby learn that Mr. Simpson is having a stag party and decide they must see the stripper. Finally, it's wedding time, but Spike and Snake are nowhere to be found.

CARELESS WHISPER

Marco and Ellie are the best of friends and maybe more. But when Marco and Ellie find themselves alone, he realizes that while he wishes he liked her that way, he doesn't. Kendra feels Toby is smothering her.

HOT FOR TEACHER

Ms. Hatzilakos gives J.T. detention — assisting her with the guinea pigs all week. If only all punishment were this good! Jimmy and Spinner's honesty pact has them at each other's throats.

MESSAGE IN A BOTTLE

While having dinner with Emma and her parents, Sean sneaks some wine in a misguided attempt to "relax." It looks like sparks are being rekindled between Ashley and Jimmy, but who will make the first move?

RELAX

When Coach Hatzilakos asks Liberty to be the floor hockey team manager, she throws all her energy into it and ends up challenging the boys' team to a game. Terri gets a shock when she reads Paige's palm.

DRESSED IN BLACK

Ashley and Jimmy are back together! It's going to be perfect this time, right? J.T. convinces Toby that they should buy condoms. But when Spinner is your girlfriend's big brother, don't let him find out!

FIGHT FOR YOUR RIGHT

Emma's latest crusade involves banning genetically modified foods from the cafeteria — which leads to a real food fight and trouble for Emma. Spinner has his heart set on an expensive designer shirt.

HOW SOON IS NOW?

Paige is sure she's recovered from her date rape. But when she finds out Dean is coming to Degrassi for a tournament, she goes into a tailspin. Ellie and Marco attempt to co-direct a commercial for class.

TEARS ARE NOT ENOUGH, PART 1

Craig goes to his dad for help with science. But old patterns re-emerge and Craig vows to get out of his father's life for good. Liberty agrees to tutor J.T. — if he will be her date for the dance.

TEARS ARE NOT ENOUGH, PART 2

Craig's wish is granted when his father is killed in a car crash — and Craig feels nothing. Paige and Spinner are determined to be the luau king and queen — over Jimmy's dead body!

SEASON 3

FATHER FIGURE, PART 1

The pending birth of Emma's new sibling sends her on a search for her birth father — and leads to a shocking discovery. Spinner decides the perfect present for Paige would be a locker in the "good" hall.

FATHER FIGURE, PART 2

When Shane turns up at Emma's, things get scary, as Spike goes into labor. Spinner's locker plans take a downturn when Jimmy makes him admit he's whipped — in public, in front of Paige.

U GOT THE LOOK

Manny is riding high on her newfound popularity and her new look, causing friction with best friend, Emma. Joey's just a little too thrilled when Craig and the guys form a band.

PRIDE, PART 1

Ellie is tired of pretending to be Marco's girlfriend and "breaks up" with him. When Spinner tries to set him up with Hazel, Marco blurts out that he's gay, and Spinner turns against him.

PRIDE, PART 2

Lost downtown, Marco is beaten up by gay-bashers. To protect baby Jack, Snake crashes with Joey when he comes down with a cold. But is there more going on than just a cold?

GANGSTA GANGSTA

Sean is torn between good girl Emma and a more daring bunch of friends who drive him to steal a laptop from Mr. Simpson. Toby spills an embarrassing secret about J.T. and his dream about Liberty.

SHOULD I STAY OR SHOULD I GO?

To keep Craig's interest, Ashley decides to have sex with him. When the secret comes out at Ashley's party, Manny moves in on Craig. Joey vows to pull Snake out of his depression and reunite The Zit Remedy.

WHISPER TO A SCREAM

Ellie has a chance at a great co-op placement, but Paige wants it, too. With everything going on in her life, Ellie just needs an outlet for her pain. Terri has a secret admirer. Could it be Toby?

AGAINST ALL ODDS

Manny and Emma sneak out to a rave where Emma might hook up with Chris. Manny ditches Emma for Craig. At a sleepover, Spinner is afraid that Marco has a crush on him.

NEVER GONNA GIVE YOU UP

Hazel doesn't like Terri's new boyfriend, Rick. Craig recognizes the hallmarks of an abuser, especially when Terri shows up with unexplained cuts and bruises. Spinner and J.T. start a prank war.

HOLIDAY: A DEGRASSI SPECIAL

Both Joey and Craig have two girls on a string as Christmas approaches. Caitlin is given a fantastic opportunity at work — just when things are heating up with Joey! Manny wants Craig to break up with Ashley. But Ashley gets a shock when she does a little snooping into Craig's Christmas present purchases. Caitlin makes a last-minute decision.

THIS CHARMING MAN

Emma is sure she's over Sean, but when she hears he was the one who stole Mr. Simpson's laptop, she is determined to get Sean in trouble. Spinner and Paige hit some bumps over their driving instructor.

ACCIDENTS WILL HAPPEN, PART 1

The big gymnastics meet is coming up, but Manny's feeling sick. And she's not positive she and Craig used protection. Could she be pregnant? Toby sets out to prove he's cool enough to hang with Jimmy.

ACCIDENTS WILL HAPPEN, PART 2

Manny faces tough choices about her pregnancy and it doesn't help that Craig has gone all mushy and wants to be a dad. Liberty develops a crush on Sean, who takes tough steps to discourage her.

TAKE ON ME

Sean, Ellie, Hazel, Jimmy, and Toby find themselves stuck together in Mr. Raditch's new Saturday detention. Ellie and Sean start to become close. Mr. Simpson gives Mr. Raditch a new perspective.

DON'T DREAM IT'S OVER

Rick makes a concerted effort to win Terri back, and she bends. It all leads to a horrible fight with Paige and then a tragic one with Rick. Ellie goes out with Sean, but drags Marco along as a security blanket.

ROCK AND ROLL HIGH SCHOOL

It's all-out war when Craig and Ashley compete in a battle of the bands. Winning the contest means everything to each of them. Caitlin baby-sits Angela and spoils her.

IT'S RAINING MEN

Marco is beyond nervous as he gets Spinner's help to prepare for his date with Dylan — which does not go as planned. J.T. is in a terrible commercial and has to deal with the teasing.

I WANT CANDY

Paige and Spinner decide to skip school for the day and bring Ashley along to cheer her up — but she's more likely to bring everyone else down! Emma discovers Snake's will and fears the worst.

OUR HOUSE

When his brother gets a job in Alberta, Sean realizes it's legal for him to stay behind and live on his own. Soon his place becomes party central. J.T. tries to ask Manny to a dance.

SEASON 4

THE POWER OF LOVE

It's the year-end semi-formal and Marco is stressing over every detail. The evening is ruined for him when his decorations catch fire and the dance moves to the parking lot. Jimmy tries to impress Hazel.

GHOST IN THE MACHINE, PART 1

Paige's court case against Dean comes to trial and she's ready to put it behind her once justice is served. Craig receives an astonishing birthday gift from his late father — $10,000!

GHOST IN THE MACHINE, PART 2

Paige is devastated when Dean is acquitted. Marco coaxes her out to a party she's not ready for. A rash and violent act nearly puts an end to Paige's relationship with Spinner. Craig buys a new guitar.

KING OF PAIN

Marco's a shoo-in for student council president until Alex enters the race, threatening to "out" him at an assembly his parents will be attending. Liberty has a crush on Chris.

MERCY STREET

Emma starts a campaign to shun Terri's abusive ex-boyfriend, Rick. But when the protest goes too far, she has to make a choice. J.T. tries a penis pump to make himself more attractive to Manny.

ANYWHERE I LAY MY HEAD

Sean invites Ellie to move in with him, but she's not sure she can abandon her alcoholic mother. Spinner helps out at the cheerleaders' car wash and gets flirty with Manny.

ISLANDS IN THE STREAM

Paige is so upset about damaging Spinner's car that she's letting him walk all over her — until she finds out about him and Manny. Toby and Rick have a friendly competition.

TIME STANDS STILL, PART 1

Jimmy ends up on the "Whack Your Brain" team with Rick and realizes that he and his friends have taken their anti-Rick campaign too far. But the others won't back off. Joey must sell his house.

TIME STANDS STILL, PART 2

Still covered in paint and feathers, Rick returns to school with a gun and a plan for revenge. Jimmy is shot and Emma could be next. But Sean steps in and the gun goes off — leaving Rick dead.

BACK IN BLACK

Sean is seen as the hero of the school shooting. He takes off with the gang to his old home of Wasaga Beach, where his past catches up to him in an unexpected way. Toby deals with Rick's death.

NEUTRON DANCE

Craig causes tension in the band when he brings in Ashley to replace Jimmy. Paige's stress level seems improved by yoga, but it's the instructor — the new student teacher — more than the yoga that's helping the most.

VOICES CARRY, PART 1

Now that Craig and Ashley are back together, Craig is determined nothing will go wrong. Everything's perfect and he couldn't be happier — until Ashley turns down his marriage proposal. Liberty and J.T. try to pull the school play together.

VOICES CARRY, PART 2

When Ashley's answer to Craig's marriage proposal changes to "not never," Craig is over the moon. Joey worries about Craig's wild mood swings. J.T. and Liberty face off against Mr. Raditch over the school play.

BARK AT THE MOON

In the wake of the shooting, Mr. Raditch is assigned to another school. New kid Chester suggests a "Cupid dance" as a way of bringing fun back to Degrassi. Spinner and Manny are becoming closer, but Manny is afraid of being part of a couple.

SECRET, PART 1

Emma has not been the same since the shooting. The school play is one distraction, going to the ravine is another, until her parents catch her sneaking in at 2:00 a.m. Ashley worries about Craig being bipolar and wants him to join a teen support group.

SECRET, PART 2

Emma is going from bad to worse as she gets involved with Jay. It's not "real" sex, right? Jimmy is going nuts in the rehab center, so Craig and Marco spring him for a concert by the one and only Kid Elrick.

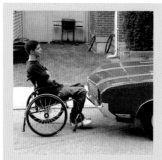

EYE OF THE TIGER

Jimmy is back, and Spinner will do anything to make up with his friend — even admitting to his part in the paint and feathers incident with Rick. Liberty's brother Daniel causes trouble between her and J.T.

QUEEN OF HEARTS

Ellie hates taking money from her mom to pay the rent. When she discovers a knack for cards, things seem to take a turn for the better. It's heating up between Paige and Matt (oops!) — Mr. Oleander!

LOVE WILL TEAR US APART

Paige and Mr. Oleander find their secret hard to keep. Emma takes heat from Chris about the ravine. Chester and his brothers turn out to be Emma's new neighbors — apparently hot new guys come in threes!

MOONLIGHT DESIRES

Spinner takes responsibility for his role in Jimmy's injury, but when no one will accept his apology, he turns on the school itself. Marco is sure he has an ally in Caitlin when the Blood Drive won't accept him — but to make things worse, Dylan won't, either.

WEST END GIRLS

Paige's bossiness around the spirit squad is not appreciated, and Manny's leadership skills begin to emerge. Cult movie director Kevin Smith searches for a school to be the set of his newest film.

GOING DOWN THE ROAD, PART 1

Ashley's dream job will split her from Craig for the summer. Kevin Smith begins filming *Jay and Silent Bob Go Canadian, Eh?* and develops a friendship with Caitlin.

GOING DOWN THE ROAD, PART 2

Craig finds out that life on his own isn't as much on his own terms as he thought it would be, especially since he has such a fine guitar. Caitlin has trouble figuring out what her heart is really telling her.

The "Going Down the Road" Title

Although songs with this title exist, and some were even released in the eighties, quite honestly, this episode's title is not from the name of an eighties pop tune. The inspiration came from a seminal 1970 Canadian film, Goin' Down the Road. It added to the "Canadiana" feel of the two season-ending episodes.

ACKNOWLEDGMENTS

I would like to thank everyone in the book, of course. Everyone at Alexander Mackenzie High School, especially my 2004–2005 students and my colleagues in the English Department for putting up with me! My family and friends for letting me off the hook. Everyone at Epitome and Madison Press who worked so hard to make this happen, and smooth my way, especially my tireless editor, Catherine Fraccaro. Linda, for hiring me in the first place. McD for his inspiration. Yan, for the love, support, and meals! — *Kathryn Ellis*

Madison Press Books would like to thank Sarah Barrable-Tishauer and Aubrey Graham for taking the time to film presentation videos for this book; Stephanie Cohen, Epitome's Director of Communications/Marketing, for joining the dance without missing a step; Adrienne Fine-Furneaux for her amazing work during the initial stages and also later on in the process; Nicole Hamilton, associate producer of *Degrassi: The Next Generation*, for being our facilitator par excellence; Mireille Majoor for getting our editorial motor running at the very beginning; Meeri Park Cunniff at Noggin/The N for her unending enthusiasm and support; Dolly Shanthakumar, once Epitome's assistant to the executive producers, now in post-production at TNG, and Sarah Timmins, Epitome's photo researcher, for their efficient and cheerful help whenever we needed it, which was often; and Kevin Watson at the CTV Television Network, for making good things happen, and quickly at that. A special thank you goes out to those who contibuted photos from their personal collections.

Playing With Time Inc. and Epitome Pictures Inc. would like to thank the many private individuals who provided financial assistance, particularly in the early days, and the many institutions that provided financial assistance to the production of *The Kids of Degrassi Street*, *Degrassi Junior High*, *Degrassi High*, *School's Out!*, *Degrassi Talks*, *Degrassi: The Next Generation*, and degrassi.tv throughout the years, including CTV Television Network, The N, Canadian Broadcasting Corporation, Canadian Television Fund, Telefilm Canada, Shaw Rocket Fund, Dr. Geoffrey R. Conway Fund, Independent Production Fund, Ontario Arts Council, United States Corporation for Public Broadcasting, WGBH Boston, Alliance Atlantis, Isme Bennie International, McNabb & Connolly, Magic Lantern, Government of Canada, Government of Ontario, Ontario Media Development Corporation, Mountain Cable Program, Snap Media, COGECO Program Development Fund, Bell Broadcast and New Media Fund, Telefilm Canada New Media Fund, Rogers Telefund, and RBC Royal Bank.

PICTURE CREDITS

Every effort has been made to correctly attribute all material reproduced in this book. If any errors have unwittingly occurred, we will be happy to correct them in future editions.

All photographs, unless otherwise designated, are courtesy of Epitome Pictures. Photographers are listed where this information was available.

Preface: page 4: courtesy Kathryn Ellis; page 5: episode shots: Janet Webb; photo of Kathryn and Amanda: courtesy Amanda Stepto; photo of Kathryn and Pat: courtesy Kathryn Ellis

Introduction: page 7: Stephen Scott

Chapter 1: pages 8, 9, and 10: courtesy Epitome Pictures; page 13: reunion photo: courtesy Sara Holmes MacGregor; TNG Season 1 group photo: courtesy Sarah

Barrable-Tishauer; pages 14 and 15: workshop photos Maria Wall; tutor with Colleen Lam: courtesy Colleen Lam; pages 16, 17, 18, and 19: then photos: Janet Webb; now photos: Kathryn Ellis

Chapter 2: pages 23, 24, and 25: Janet Webb

Chapter 3: page 27: John Bertram; page 28: then photos: Janet Webb; now photos: courtesy Dayo Ade and David Armin Parcells; page 29: then photos: Janet Webb; now photo of Danah-Jean Brown: courtesy Colleen Lam; page 30, then photos: Janet Webb except Christian Campbell: courtesy Kathryn Ellis; now photos: Darrin Brown: courtesy Colleen Lam; Christian Campbell: ©Jeff Vespa, courtesy Christian Campbell; Michael Carry: courtesy Sara Holmes MacGregor; Andy Chambers: courtesy Andy Chambers;

page 31: then photos: Janet Webb; Sarah Charlesworth: courtesy Colleen Lam; now photos: Danny Ciraco: courtesy Danny Ciraco; Irene Courakos: courtesy: Sara Holmes MacGregor; page 32: then photos: Janet Webb; now photos: Sabrina Dias: courtesy Sabrina Dias; page 33: then photos: Janet Webb except Craig Driscoll: courtesy Colleen Lam; Marsha Ferguson: courtesy Kathryn Ellis; now photos: Chrisa Erodotou: courtesy Maureen McKay; Cameron Graham: courtesy Colleen Lam; Anais Granofsky: courtesy Sara Holmes MacGregor; page 34: then photos: Janet Webb; now photos: Sara Holmes: courtesy Sara Holmes MacGregor; Jacy Hunter: courtesy Jacy Hunter; page 35: then photos: Janet Webb except Dean Ifill: courtesy Kathryn Ellis; now photos: Dean Ifill: courtesy Colleen Lam; Andy Jekabsons: courtesy Andy Jekabsons; Anna Keenan: courtesy Cathy Keenan; page 36:

then photos: Janet Webb except Cathy Keenan: T. Thorne; Kyra Levy: courtesy Kathryn Ellis; now photos, Cathy Keenan: courtesy Cathy Keenan; Niki Kemeny: courtesy Niki Kemeny; Colleen Lam: courtesy Colleen Lam; Kyra Levy: courtesy Sara Holmes MacGregor; page 37: then photos: Janet Webb; now photos: Arlene Lott: courtesy Arlene Lott; Maureen McKay: courtesy Maureen McKay; Siluck Saysanasy: courtesy Sarah Barrable-Tishauer; page 38: then photos: Janet Webb except Nicole Stoffman: Maria Wall; now photos: Karryn Sheridan: courtesy Karryn Sheridan; Nicole Stoffman: courtesy Nicole Stoffman; Vincent Walsh: courtesy Vincent Walsh; page 39, then photos: Janet Webb except Lisa Williams: courtesy Colleen Lam; now photos, Lisa Williams: courtesy Colleen Lam; Michelle Goodeve: courtesy Michelle Goodeve; pages 40 and 41: Barbara Cole; page 42: Fred Phipps; page 43: Christos Kalohoridis; page 44: Steve Wilkie; page 45: Janet Webb; page 46: Janet Webb; page 47: Christos Kalohoridis; page 48: Christos Kalohoridis; pages 49, 50, and 51: Janet Webb; page 52: left and right: courtesy Sarah Barrable-Tishauer; center: Stephen Scott; page 53: young Sarah, Sarah with Ryan Cooley, Sarah with Gregory Hines: courtesy Sarah Barrable-Tishauer; episodes, bottom left: Stephen Scott, bottom center: Steve Wilkie; page 54: Steve Wilkie; young Daniel: Steve Wilkie, courtesy Corus Entertainment Inc.; page 55: left: Steve Wilkie, courtesy Corus Entertainment Inc.; center: Jennifer Lum; right: Ken Woroner; page 56: left: Stephen Scott; young Lauren: Steve Wilkie, courtesy Corus Entertainment Inc; center: Christos Kalohoridis; far right: Stephen Scott; page 57: left: Chris Jackson; center: Barbara Cole; page 58: Steve Wilkie, courtesy Corus Entertainment Inc.; page 59: top: courtesy Amanda Stepto; center: Barbara Cole; bottom: Steve Wilkie, courtesy Corus Entertainment Inc; Kraft dinner: Jennifer Lum; page 60: Steve Wilkie, Christos Kalohoridis; dice: Jennifer Lum; page 61: Stephen Scott; Rick with glasses: Sarah Barrable-Tishauer; page 62: young Jake: courtesy Jake Epstein; Jake as the Artful Dodger: © National Post/Chris Bolin; page 63: Steve Wilkie; Barbara Cole; page 64: top: Chris Jackson; bottom:

Ken Woroner; collar: Jennifer Lum; page 65: top: Barbara Cole; bottom: Stephen Scott; page 67: top left: courtesy Susie Waldman; top right: courtesy Cassie Steele; bottom left: courtesy Susie Waldman; bottom center: Steve Wilkie; bottom right: courtesy Cassie Steele; computer: Jennifer Lum; page 68: top: Christos Kalohoridis; bottom: Steve Wilkie; page 69: top: Steve Wilkie; bottom: Barbara Cole; page 70: left: Chris Jackson; right: Barbara Cole; page 71: right: Steve Wilkie; page 72: left: Christos Kalohoridis; right: courtesy Andrea Lewis; page 73: left: courtesy Andrea Lewis; right: Stephen Scott; microphone: Jennifer Lum; page 74: purses: Jennifer Lum; page 75: top left: Stephen Scott; top right: Steve Wilkie; bottom right: Barbara Cole; page 76: top: courtesy Melissa McIntyre; center and bottom: Steve Wilkie; page 77: top: Chris Jackson; center: Christos Kaholoridis; bottom: Mike Courtney; page 78: combs: Jennifer Lum; page 79: top left: Christos Kaholoridis/Steve Wilkie; top right: Barbara Cole; bottom left: Steve Wilkie; bottom right: Chris Jackson; page 80: top: Steve Wilkie; bottom: courtesy Cassie Steele; page 81: top and center: courtesy Cassie Steele; bottom: Stephen Scott; page 82: all courtesy Sarah Barrable-Tishauer; page 83: top: Steve Wilkie; center: Christos Kaholoridis; bottom: courtesy John Bregar; page 84: top and center: Stephen Scott; bottom: Steve Wilkie; page 85: left: Stephen Scott; center: Steve Wilkie; right: Barbara Cole; page 86: top and bottom: Steve Wilkie; page 87: top: Sarah Barrable-Tishauer; bottom: Chris Jackson; page 88: top: Mike Courtney; bottom: Christos Kaholoridis; page 89: top: courtesy Alex Steele; bottom: Stephen Scott; page 90: top left: Stephen Scott; top right: courtesy Tom Melissis; bottom left: Cylla Von Tiedemann; bottom right: courtesy Jennifer Podemski; page 91: top right: Steve Wilkie; bottom: Stephen Scott; page 92: center: John Bertram; bottom: Janet Webb; page 93: Cylla Von Tiedemann; Christos Kalohoridis; Kalohoridis/Wilkie; Steve Wilkie; Stephen Scott; page 94: top two: John Bertram; remaining: Janet Webb; page 95: top: Janet Webb; next two photos: Stephen Scott; Mike Courtney; Cylla Von Tiedemann; Janet Webb

Chapter 4: pages 97, 98, and 99: Kathryn Ellis, except Anais directs: Mike Courtney; page 100; Stephen Scott; page 101: Steve Wilkie; page 103: top photo: Stephen Scott; bottom photo: Kathryn Ellis; pages 104 and 105; Kathryn Ellis; page 106: group photo: Janet Webb; Vincent Massey High School: Lisa Cardile; pages 107, 108, 109, and 110: then photos: Janet Webb; now photos: Lisa Cardile; page 111: homes: Lisa Cardile; Centennial College: Kathryn Ellis; Danforth Avenue sign: Donna Chong; pages 112 and 113: Jennifer Lum; page 114: top left: Mike Courtney; top center: courtesy Epitome Pictures; top right: Stephen Scott; bottom left: Jennifer Lum; bottom center: Stephen Scott; bottom right: Kathryn Ellis; page 115: all Jennifer Lum; page 116: Stephen Scott; page 117: all Jennifer Lum; pages 118 and 119: Janet Webb, courtesy Judy Shiner Toker; page 121: Stephen Stanley; page 122: top photo: Chris Jackson; bottom photo: courtesy Cassie Steele; page 123: top and bottom: Chris Jackson; page 124: Janet Webb; page 125: young Caitlin: Janet Webb; far right: Stephen Scott; page 126: courtesy Lewis Manne and Wendy Watson; page 127: Janet Webb and Fred Phipps; page 128: courtesy Jody Colero; page 129: photo of Jim: courtesy Jim McGrath; photos of Ashley and Craig: Steve Wilkie; page 130: top: Fred Phipps; bottom: Christos Kalohoridis; page 131: all Christos Kalohoridis; page 132: Janet Webb; page 133: top: Jennifer Lum; posters, courtesy Epitome Pictures; bottom photo: Janet Webb

Chapter 5: page 134: Christos Kalohoridis; page 153: top: Steve Wilkie; center: Mike Courtney; bottom: Janet Webb; page 136: Steve Wilkie; page 137: Janet Webb; page 138: top: Christos Kalohoridis; bottom left: Janet Webb; bottom right: Mike Courtney; page 139: top: Janet Webb; bottom: Mike Courtney; page 140: top: Stephen Scott; center and bottom and page 141: courtesy Epitome Pictures

Chapter 6: page 142: courtesy Kathryn Ellis; page 143: top: courtesy Kathryn Ellis; Amanda Stepto in London, courtesy Amanda Stepto; TNG tour photos, courtesy

Epitome Pictures; page 144: top: courtesy Miriam McDonald; jacket photo: Jennifer Lum, jacket: courtesy Kathryn Ellis; page 145: courtesy Epitome Pictures; page 147: Dot Grill: Jennifer Lum

Chapter 7: page 148: Janet Webb; page 149: Queen's University Degrassi party photo, courtesy Mark Janson; The Zit Remedy, Fred Phipps; page 150: clockwise from top left: courtesy Sarah Barrable-Tishauer; courtesy Miriam McDonald; courtesy Colleen Lam; courtesy Sarah Barrable-Tishauer; courtesy Colleen Lam; courtesy Arlene Lott; page 151: clockwise from top left: courtesy Colleen Lam; courtesy Amanda Stepto; courtesy Susie Waldman; invitations courtesy Sarah Barrable-Tishauer; courtesy Kathryn Ellis; Imoinda Romain; page 152: courtesy Miriam McDonald; page 153: top left and right: Janet Webb; center: courtesy Kathryn Ellis; bottom: courtesy Colleen Lam

Chapter 8: pages 154 to 158: John Bertram; page 159: Kiss Me Steph: Maria Wall; remaining through page 161: Janet Webb/John Bertram; page 161 Season 2 through page 172: all Janet Webb, except page 172: group photo,

Fred Phipps; page 173 through 175: Janet Webb/Laura Vickers; page 176: all Cylla Von Tiedemann; page 177: all Mike Courtney except Parents' Day: Cylla Von Tiedemann; page 178: Rumors and Reputation, Under Pressure, Jagged Little Pill: Mike Courtney; Friday Night, Cabaret: Cylla Von Tiedemann; page 179: all Mike Courtney; page 180: all Mike Courtney except Shout, Part 2: Christos Kalohoridis; page 181: all Mike Courtney, except Message in a Bottle, Relax, Dressed in Black: David Griffith; page 182: all Mike Courtney, except Father Figure, Part 1 and U Got the Look: Steve Wilkie and Father Figure, Part 2: Christos Kalohoridis; page 183: Pride, Part 1 and Part 2: Christos Kalohoridis; Gangsta, Gangsta, Whisper to a Scream, Against All Odds: Steve Wilkie; page 184: Accidents Will Happen, Part 1: Steve Wilkie; Accidents Will Happen, Part 2: Christos Kalohoridis; page 185: all Christos Kalohoridis except Our House: Ken Woroner; page 186: The Power of Love: Kalohoridis/Wilkie; Ghost in the Machine, Part 1: Steve Wilkie; remaining photos: Stephen Scott; page 187: all Steve Wilkie; page 188: Voices Carry, Part 2, Secret, Part 2, Eye of the Tiger:

Steve Wilkie; Bark at the Moon, Secret, Part 1, Queen of Hearts: Stephen Scott; page 189: Moonlight Desires, West End Girls: Steve Wilkie; Love Will Tear Us Apart, Going Down the Road, Part 1 and Part 2: Stephen Scott

SONG CREDITS

"Whatever It Takes" (Theme to *Degrassi: The Next Generation*) written by Jody Colero, Jim McGrath, and Stephen Stohn © 2001 Silent Joe, Jim McGrath & Ellipse Media Consulting Corp. All rights reserved. Administered by Peermusic Canada, Inc. Used under license.

Degrassi Junior High Theme Song written by Wendy Watson and Lewis Manne © 1985 Fatwatson Music & Manimal Music (SOCAN). All rights reserved. Used under license.

Degrassi High Theme Song written by Wendy Watson and Lewis Manne © 1985 & 1988 Fatwatson Music & Manimal Music (SOCAN). All rights reserved. Used under license.

DEGRASSI: GENERATIONS
was produced by

MADISON PRESS BOOKS
1000 Yonge Street, Suite 200
Toronto, Ontario, Canada
M4W 2K2
www.madisonpressbooks.com

Project Editor: Catherine Fraccaro
Executive Editor: Imoinda Romain
Editorial Assistance: Shima Aoki
Editorial Director: Wanda Nowakowska

Art Director: Jennifer Lum
Designer: Diana Sullada

Production Managers: Donna Chong, Sandra L. Hall
Production Director: Susan Barrable

Director, Business Development: Christopher Jackson
Publisher: Oliver Salzmann

Printed in Singapore by Imago Productions (F.E.) Ltd., Singapore